The GOLD
SEEKERS

Nancy Roberts

The GOLD SEEKERS

Gold, Ghosts and Legends from Carolina to California

University of South Carolina Press

Published in Columbia, South Carolina, by the
University of South Carolina Press

Manufactured in the United States of America

99 98 97 96   5 4 3 2

ISBN 0–87249–657–0
      0–87249–658–9 (pbk.)

Library of Congress Catalog Card No. 89–22563

Contents

Acknowledgments vii

Fact and Fiction ix

Introduction 1

I. TALES OF THE SOUTHEASTERN GOLD RUSHES

  1. The Discovery of Gold in North Carolina 7

  2. The Specter of the Reed Mine 28

  3. The Legendary Walter George 36

  4. The Grisly Ghost of Gold Hill 49

  5. The Discovery of Gold in Virginia 55

  6. The Discovery of Gold in South Carolina 63

  7. They Called Me "Fool Billy" 68

  8. Scarlett O'Hara of the Dorn Mine 76

  9. The Future of Cap'n Thies 86

  10. The Discovery of Gold in Georgia 98

  11. "Free Jim" 112

  12. Old Miss Mollie's Back 138

  13. The Discovery of Gold in Alabama 147

II. **TALES OF THE WESTERN GOLD RUSHES**

    14.   The Discovery of Gold in California   155

    15.   A North Carolinian Shapes California   169

    16.   Off to the Gold Rush   179

    17.   Green Russell: A Man Without Fear   192

    18.   Darling of the Gold Camps   222

    19.   The Bride of Vallecito   239

    20.   The Mark of Black Bart   247

Acknowledgments

Bancroft Library, University of California, Berkeley, California 94720

The Carolina Gold Rush: America's First, by Bruce Roberts. S&L Sales, Industrial Boulevard, Waycross, Georgia (Donation of Bruce Roberts photos)

Colorado Historical Society, 1300 Broadway, Denver, Colorado 80203

Denver Public Library, 1357 Broadway, Denver, Colorado 80203-2165

Hodge, Robert A., 417 Pelham Street, Fredericksburg, Virginia 22401 (Virginia Gold Rush)

Hunter, Richard E., Jr., Clerk of Court, Warrenton, North Carolina (General Thomas J. Green, will)

Le Fevre, Byron and Vera, Dahlonega, Georgia

North Carolina State Archives, Raleigh, North Carolina (*Harper's Monthly* sketches)

William R. Perkins Library, Duke University, Durham, North Carolina (Manuscript Department, Adeline Ellery Davis Green Papers)

Southern Historical Collection, University of North Carolina, Chapel Hill, North Carolina (Manuscript Department, Horn Papers)

University of Texas Press, Austin, Texas (Map of Russell brothers' trips West)

Division of Mineral Resources, Natural Resources Building, McCormick Road, Charlottesville, Virginia 22903

Virginia State Library, Twelfth & Capitol Streets, Richmond, Virginia 25219

Fact and Fiction

This book strives for an honest blend of history and fiction and the reader is entitled to know which is which.

1. THE DISCOVERY OF GOLD IN NORTH CAROLINA
Based on historical fact.
Sources

Asbury, Daniel. "Gold Mines at Gold Hill, Rowan County, N.C." *Mining Magazine*, Vol. 1 1853.

Becker, G. F. "Reconnaissance of the Gold Fields of the Southern Appalachians." U.S. Geological Survey, 16th Annual Report, 1894, pt. 3, pp. 251–319.

Boyd, William K. *History of North Carolina: The Federal Period, 1783–1860.* Lewis Publishing Company, Chicago and New York, 1919.

Glass, Brent D. "King Midas and the Old Rip: The Gold Hill Mining District of North Carolina." Doctoral Dissertation, University of North Carolina.

Green, Fletcher M. "Gold Mining: A Forgotten Industry of Ante-Bellum North Carolina." *The North Carolina Historical Review*, Vol. XLV, Jan. 1937, Number 1.

Hurley, Thomas Jefferson. *Famous Gold Nuggets of the World.* Doubleday, New York, 1900.

Knapp, Richard F. "Golden Promise in the Piedmont: The Story of John Reed's Mine." Division of Archives and History, North Carolina Department of Cultural Resources, 1975.

Nitze, H. B. C. "Gold mining in the Southern States." *Engineering Magazine*, Vol. 10, 1896.

Nitze, H. B. C. and G. B. Hanna. "Gold Deposits of North Carolina." North Carolina Geological Survey, Bulletin 3, 1896.

Nitze, H. B. C. and H. A. J. Wilkins. "Gold Mining in North Carolina and Adjacent South Appalachian Regions." North Carolina Geological Survey, Bulletin 10, 1897.

Pardee, J. T. and C. F. Park, Jr. "Gold Deposits of the Southern Piedmont." U.S. Department of the Interior, Geological Survey, Professional Paper 213, 1948.

Roberts, Bruce. The Carolina Gold Rush: America's First. McNally and Loftin, Publishers, Charlotte, N.C., 1971.

2. THE SPECTER OF THE REED MINE
A ghost story based on the legend about Engine Shaft at the Reed Gold Mine, North Carolina State Historic Site near Charlotte, North Carolina.

3. THE LEGENDARY WALTER GEORGE
Based on historical fact.
Sources
Glass, Brent D. "King Midas and the Old Rip: The Gold Hill Mining District of North Carolina." Doctoral Dissertation, University of North Carolina.

Laney, F. B. "The Gold Hill Mining District of North Carolina." North Carolina Geological Survey, Bulletin 21, 1910.

"The Gold Fields of North Carolina." Prospectus, North Carolina Gold Mining and Bullion Co., 18 Wall Street, New York City. Issued Oct. 1, 1891.

Roberts, Bruce. The Carolina Gold Rush: America's First. McNally and Loftin, Publishers, Charlotte, N.C., 1971.

4. THE GRISLY GHOST OF GOLD HILL
A ghost story based on local lore.

5. THE DISCOVERY OF GOLD IN VIRGINIA
Based on historical fact.
Sources
Becker, G. F. "Reconnaissance of the Gold Fields of the Southern Appalachians." U.S. Geological Survey, 16th Annual Report, 1894.

Green, Fletcher M. "Gold Mining in Ante-Bellum Virginia. *The Virginia Magazine of History and Biography.* Vol. XLV, July 1937, No. 3.

Sweet, Palmer C. "Gold in Virginia." Virginia Division of Mineral Resources, Publication 19, 1980.

_____. "Processes of Gold Recovery in Virginia." *Virginia Minerals,* Vol. 26, Aug. 1980, No. 3.

_____. "Gold mines and prospects in Virginia." *Virginia Minerals,* Vol. 17, Aug. 1971, No. 1.

_____. "Road Log to some abandoned gold mines of the Gold-Pyrite Belt, Northeastern Virginia." *Virginia Minerals,* Vol. 21, Feb. 1975, No. 1.

6. THE DISCOVERY OF GOLD IN SOUTH CAROLINA
Based on historical fact.
Sources
Bradt, Harlan H., and Edmund Newton. "Gold Mining at the Haile Mine in South Carolina." *Mining Congress Journal,* Oct. 1938.

Lieber, O. M. Fourth Annual Report on the Survey of South Carolina (for 1859), (1860).

McCauley, Camilla K., and J. Robert Butler. "Gold Resources of South Carolina." Division of Geology, South Carolina State Development Board, Bulletin 32, 1966.

Nitze, H. B. C. "Gold mining in the Southern States." *Engineering Magazine,* Vol. 10, 1896.

Nitze, H. B. C. and H. A. J. Wilkins. "Gold Mining in North Carolina and Adjacent South Appalachian Regions." North Carolina Geological Survey, Bulletin 10, 1897.

Pardee, J. T. and C. F. Park, Jr. "Gold Deposits of the Southern Piedmont." U.S. Department of the Interior, Geological Survey, Professional Paper 213, 1948.

Roberts, Bruce. "The Carolina Gold Rush: America's First. McNally and Loftin, Publishers, Charlotte, N.C., 1971.

7. THEY CALLED ME "FOOL BILLY"
A first person fictional account based on historical fact.

Sources

Marschalk, Susan. "Gold Fever!" ("Fool" Billy Dorn) *The Spectator Magazine.* Clipping files of the McCormick County Library, McCormick, S. C.

McCauley, Camilla K., and J. Robert Butler. "Gold Resources of South Carolina." Division of Geology, South Carolina State Development Board, Bulletin 32, 1966.

Pardee, J. T. and C. F. Park, Jr. "Gold Deposits of the Southern Piedmont." U.S. Department of the Interior, Geological Survey, Professional Paper 213, 1948.

8. SCARLETT O'HARA OF THE DORN MINE

A ghost story based on local lore.

9. THE FUTURE OF CAP'N THIES

Based on historical fact with the exception of characters' thoughts and emotions.

Sources

McCauley, Camilla K., and J. Robert Butler. "Gold Resources of South Carolina." Division of Geology, South Carolina State Development Board, Bulletin 32, 1966.

Nitze, H. B. C. and H. A. J. Wilkins. "Gold Mining in North Carolina and Adjacent South Appalachian Regions." North Carolina Geological Survey, Bulletin 10, 1897.

Pittman, Clyde Calhoun. "Death of a Gold Mine." R. L. Bryan Co., Columbia, S.C.

Roberts, Bruce. *The Carolina Gold Rush: America's First."* McNally and Loftin, Publishers, Charlotte, N.C., 1971.

10. THE DISCOVERY OF GOLD IN GEORGIA

Based on historical fact.

Sources

Coulter, E. Merton. *Auraria.* Athens, Georgia: The University of Georgia Press, 1956.

Green, Fletcher M. "Georgia's Forgotten Industry: Gold Mining." *The Georgia Historical Quarterly,* XIX, June 1935, Number 2.

Cain, Andrew W. History of Lumpkin County for the First Hundred Years. The Reprint Company, Publishers, Spartanburg, S.C., 1979.

Hepburn, Lawrence R. "The Georgia History Book." Institute of Government, University of Georgia, 1982.

Jackson, R. Olin. "Dahlonega." *Georgia Journal*, Vol. 4, Number 4, 1984.

Jones, S. P. "Second Report on the Gold Deposits of Georgia." Charles P. Byrd, Atlanta, 1909.

Nitze, H. B. C. "Gold mining in the Southern States." *Engineering Magazine*, Vol. 10, 1896.

Nitze, H. B. C. and H. A. J. Wilkins. "Gold Mining in North Carolina and Adjacent South Appalachian Regions." North Carolina Geological Survey, Bulletin 10, 1897.

Pardee, J. T. and C. F. Park, Jr. "Gold Deposits of the Southern Piedmont." U.S. Department of the Interior, Geological Survey, Professional Paper 213, 1948.

Yeates, W. S. "A Preliminary Report on a Part of the Gold Deposits of Georgia." Franklin Printing and Publishing Company, Atlanta.

11. "FREE JIM"

Major events in this man's life are based on historical fact (Augusta origin, "Free Jim" Mine, staking miners, and his death). Except for Dr. Singleton, the Mint Superintendent, and Duncan characters in this account are fictional.

12. OLD MISS MOLLIE'S BACK

A ghost story based on regional folklore.

13. THE DISCOVERY OF GOLD IN ALABAMA

Based on historical fact.

Sources

"Alabama's gold rush died when California beckoned." *Birmingham News*, Birmingham, Al., Aug. 3, 1980.

"Gullies evidence of quest for gold." *Birmingham News*, Birmingham, Al., Oct. 8, 1972.

"Paying deposits of gold worked." *Birmingham News*, Birmingham, Al., Nov. 11, 1931.

"They Are Closed Now, But S.C. Has Gold Mines." *The State*, Columbia, S.C., May 24, 1970.

"Near-ghost town remains from Alabama's gold rush." *Birmingham News*, Birmingham, Al., Dec. 9, 1973.

"Gold! Talladega County mines glittered during 1800s." *The Daily Home*, Birmingham, Al., Dec. 6, 1979.

"Stubborn Mule Leads Farm Woman To Discover Cache of Gold Nuggets." *Birmingham News*, Birmingham, Al., Sept. 13, 1938.

"Days of Gold Mining Not Gone in Alabama Hills, Streams." *Huntsville Times*, Huntsville, Al., Aug. 10, 1970.

"Gold in Alabama." Geological Survey of Alabama, Birmingham Public Library.

14. THE DISCOVERY OF GOLD IN CALIFORNIA
Based on historical fact.
Sources

Asbury, Herbert. *The Barbary Coast.* Alfred A. Knopf, Inc., 1933.

Bauer, Helen. *California Gold Days.* Doubleday & Company, Inc., Garden City, N.Y., 1954.

Bachelis, Faren Maree. *The Pelican Guide to Sacramento and the Gold Country.* Pelican Publishing Company, Gretna, La., 1987.

Crosley, Mary Edith. "Coloma: California's Golden Beginning." Coloma, Calif., 1958.

Jackson, Joseph Henry. *Anybody's Gold.* Chronicle Books, San Francisco, Calif., 1970.

Manly, William L. *Death Valley in '49.* Borden Publishing Co., Los Angeles, Calif., 1949.

Prescott, William H. *The Conquest of Mexico.* A. L. Burt Company, Publishers, New York, 1844.

Ritchie, Robert Welles. *The Hell-roarin' Forty-Niners.* J. H. Sears & Company, Inc., Publishers, New York, 1928.

Wagner, Jack R. *Gold Mines of California.* Howell-North Books, San Diego, Calif., 1970.

"Historical Sketch of Thomas Jefferson Green (1801–1863)." Southern Historical Collection, Wilson Library. University of North Carolina, Chapel Hill, N.C. (Manuscript Department, Horn Papers).

15. A NORTH CAROLINIAN SHAPES CALIFORNIA

Based on historical facts in the life of General Green. The name of Green's Mexican confederate and some of the details of his dramatic escape from Castle Perote are fictional.

Sources

Ashe, S. A. "Biographical History of North Carolina." Vol. 2. The Reprint Company, Publishers, Spartanburg, S.C., 1979.

Green, W. J. "General Thomas J. Green of Warren." *University of North Carolina Magazine,* II [no. 5].

_____. *Recollections and Reflections: An Autobiography of Half a Century and More.* (Includes sketch of life of father, General Thomas J. Green) Edwards & Broughton, Raleigh, N.C., 1906.

16. OFF TO THE GOLD RUSH

Based on historical fact using correspondence between Burr and his wife.

Sources

Burr, James. "Journal of a Cruise to California and the Diggins." Manuscript Department, Adeline Ellery Burr Davis Green Papers, William R. Perkins Library. Duke University, Durham, N.C.

"Historical Sketch of Thomas Jefferson Green (1801–1863)." Southern Historical Collection, Wilson Library. University of North Carolina, Chapel Hill, N.C. (Manuscript Department, Horn Papers).

Map of Russell brothers' trips west. University of Texas Press, Austin, Tex.

17. GREEN RUSSELL: A MAN WITHOUT FEAR
Based on historical fact.
Sources
"Russell-ing gold in Colorado." *Denver Post*, Magazine section, Nov. 24, 1985, p. 22.
"The gold that started it all." *Denver Post*, May 30, 1976.
Byrnes, James. "Green Russell." *Carbonate Weekly Chronicle*, Apr. 11, 1938. Copy in Library Files, State Historical Society of Colorado, Denver.
Cain, Andrew W. *History of Lumpkin County for the First Hundred Years.* The Reprint Company, Publishers, Spartanburg, S.C., 1979.
Fagan, T. A. "The Russell Brothers." *Denver Post*, June 23, 1901. Copy in Library Files, State Historical Society of Colorado, Denver.
Forrest, James T. *Old Fort Garland.* The State Historical Society of Colorado, Denver, 1954.
Hafen, LeRoy R. *Colorado Gold Rush: Contemporary Letters and Reports, 1858–1859.* The Arthur H. Clark Co., Glendale, Calif., 1941.
_____. *Overland Route to the Gold Fields, 1859: From Contemporary Diaries.* Glendale, Calif.: The Arthur H. Clark Co., 1942.
_____. *Pike's Peak Gold Rush Guide Books of 1859, by Luke Tierney, William B. Parsons and Summaries of the Other Fifteen.* The Arthur H. Clark Co., Glendale, Calif., 1941.
Pierce, James H. "The First Prospecting of Colorado." *The Trail*, March 1911. Copy in Library Files, State Historical Society of Colorado, Denver.
_____. "The Green Russell Party." *The Trail*, May 1921. Copy in Library Files, State Historical Society of Colorado, Denver.
Smith, Joseph Emerson. "Denver's First Christmas." *Clear Creek Mining Journal* (Idaho Springs, Co.), Dec. 25, 1953–Jan. 1, 1954.

_____. "Thirteen Stayed." *Clear Creek Mining Journal* (Idaho Springs, Co.), July 10, 1953.

Spencer, Elma Dill Russell. *Green Russell and Gold.* University of Texas Press, Austin, 1966.

Villard, Henry. *The Past and Present of the Pike's Peak Gold Regions.* Princeton University Press, Princeton, N.J., 1932.

18. DARLING OF THE GOLD CAMPS

Based on historical fact except for the fictional character of her miner friend.

Sources

Dempsey, David K. *The Triumph and Trials of Lotta Crabtree.* Morrow, N.Y., 1968.

Jackson, Joseph Henry. *Anybody's Gold.* Chronicle Books, San Francisco, Calif., 1970.

Jackson, Phyllis Wynn. *Golden Footlights: the Merrymaking Career of Lotta Crabtree.* Holiday House, N.Y., 1949.

Place, Marian T. *Lotta Crabtree; Girl of the Gold Rush.* Bobbs-Merrill, Indianapolis, 1958.

19. THE BRIDE OF VALLECITO

A ghost story based on regional folklore.

20. THE MARK OF BLACK BART

Based on historical facts in as much as it can be separated from the legends that surround this colorful bandit. The Wells Fargo men and law officers are real as is the boy hero, James Rolleri, Jr.

Sources

Doney, Harry. "The True Story of Black Bart." *Woodland Democrat*, Woodland, Calif.

Jackson, Joseph Henry. *Tintypes in Gold: Four Studies in Robbery.* Macmillan, New York City, 1939.

Jackson, Joseph Henry. *Anybody's Gold.* Chronicle Books, San Francisco, Calif., 1970.

Richards, Stanley. *Black Bart.* C. Davies. 1966. California State Library, Sacramento, Calif.

Roddy, W. Lee. "Black Bart and Other California Outlaws." Genie Printing Co., Ceres, Calif., 1970. California State Library, Sacramento, Calif.

NOTE: *In many cases, present-day names of locations are used for ease of reference.*

The GOLD SEEKERS

Introduction

This is a book about the people of both the southern and western gold fields . . . the southern where the gold rush first began . . . and those who made the trek West where gold was discovered almost half a century later. Since the presence of human beings rarely occurs without ghost lore, there are several tales of the supernatural from the gold camps.

Children have a refreshing amount of curiosity that we might do well to heed more often. So, because of a twelve-year-old boy named Conrad Reed, I have chosen the year 1799 to begin our story.

It was a warm spring morning in the fragrant pine woods of the North Carolina Piedmont, and the children were eager to go wading in Little Meadow Creek. There were fish in the clear, sparkling water and as Conrad Reed aimed a bow and arrow at one of them, a strange rock captured his interest. The rays of the sun caused it to shine so brilliantly that he squinted his eyes almost closed to look at it. Then he positioned his feet carefully upon the stones in the water, crossed to the opposite bank and, reaching down, tugged at the gleaming rock. Strain as he would, it did not budge.

The stone was far heavier than he had anticipated, and when he finally wrested it from the bank there was a sucking sound as it left the mud.

"Mmm, that's pretty! What you goin' to do with it?" his little sister asked.

"Tote it up to the house," replied Conrad matter-of-factly. His father exclaimed over the weight, friends were

1

curious about its composition but nobody knew what it was, so his mother decided to use it for a doorstop.

Three years later he prevailed upon his father to take it to the nearest trading post at Fayetteville for someone to examine. A jeweler-assayer offered John Reed the ridiculously low price of three dollars and fifty cents for a gold bar which he had made from the melted down rock and farmer Reed went home happy.

And then . . . who knows? Perhaps, a British sea captain chancing to pass through Fayetteville saw the bar, held it in his weathered hand and for it squandered almost the entire pay from his last voyage. He displayed it proudly to a wealthy merchant who was taking passage aboard his ship from the port city of Charleston, South Carolina, to England.

When he saw it the gentleman coveted it and before the voyage was over he had convinced the captain to sell him the bar in order that he might have a piece of gold jewelry designed for his fiancée in London. A month later the merchant dropped an intricate pendant made from the first native American gold into the outstretched hand of a fair English lady. Then, just as we see the curtain of the forest part for a stag and close behind it, so the southern gold rush was lost to view . . . at least to the compilers of history texts.

Little was written about native North American gold until the forty-niners but the first discovery of gold caused a mass migration into the southern states; and signs of old mines may still be seen. There are chips of milk white quartz strewn along stream banks left from old mine tailings; and there are brush heaps piled high in the midst of fields that often cover a deep and dangerous vertical shaft.

There is forest land, pitted with holes and scarred by trenches with the appearance of a battlefield but no battle ever took place there . . . only hordes of men bearing picks, shovels and gold pans who pitted themselves against red clay and rock.

This was not meant to be a book describing all the various methods of extracting gold and certainly not a collection of essays on all the states where gold has been found. It is a book about several of the earliest discoveries of this metal that drives us to such excesses, some extraordinary people and . . . the supernatural.

Of the men and women who went West all encountered adventure, a few discovered gold, and many others returned empty-handed. As Castaneda, chronicler of Coronado's expedition, wrote three hundred years earlier, "Granted they did not find the riches of which they had been told but they found a place to search for them." *A place to search* has lent zest to life from the time of the Knights of the Holy Grail to the astronauts' quest for knowledge of space.

The gold rush was "the supreme adventure" of America's early history; sometimes transforming venturesome easterners and southerners into the pioneer settlers and "first families" of many a western state. And the gold itself, brought to the new United States Mints, helped stabilize the economy of a young, cash-poor country during the first half of the nineteenth century.

So, may it be forever remembered that the great American gold rush began in the Carolinas and that California was the other end of this beneficent rainbow.

But after the height of the gold seeking frenzy was over and most of the prospectors gone, I am tempted to agree with folklorist J. Frank Dobie who wrote, "These people had nothing but hope. They were rich in it. As I grow older I wonder if any other form of wealth is more enriching to lives."

Part I:
Tales of the
Southeastern
Gold Rushes

1.
The Discovery of Gold in North Carolina

America's first gold rush began in North Carolina, not in California. It all started with John Reed and not John Sutter—by chance, each was a German immigrant. And when gold was found on their land, they both shared the same concern about their crops and were more interested in farming than mining. But here similarities end.

Sutter was born in 1803, one year after John Reed stood in Little Meadow Creek surveying a stream on his farm in which millions of dollars worth of gold lay glittering just below the water's surface. The North Carolina gold rush was a small-scale version of what happened in California and fate had cast just as unlikely a man in the lead role.

John Reed was born in Darmstadt, Germany, in January of 1758. He had the misfortune of being conscripted into the army of Prince Frederick and loaned to the king of England to fight the American colonists. Reed arrived sometime during the winter of 1778 to 1779 and shortly afterwards left Long Island, New York, with British, Hessian, and Tory units to take part in the capture of Charleston, South Carolina. But he felt a deep sympathy with the colonists and resented being forced to fight for what he thought was an unjust cause.

Attempting to escape, he was caught by the British and given thirty-nine lashes as punishment. Apparently in a state of euphoria after the capture of Charleston, they dealt with this insubordinate deserter in a most unusual fashion. After his punishment they simply told Reed to "go to the devil" and they washed their hands of him. He went to

Cabarrus County, North Carolina, where there were German settlers. John Reed spoke English poorly, so it was no wonder that he was attracted to a German-speaking settlement.

He was in a strange country but he had farmed as a boy and started farming once more; in fact, by the time Cornwallis had surrendered at Yorktown, John Reed was already saving his money toward the purchase of land. In 1799 the farm houses of Mecklenburg and the surrounding counties were far apart, the land sparsely settled and desolate.

A Cornishman in the piney woods of Davidson County wrote, "I have been in dense tropical forests, on the silent plains of South America, on the equally silent steppes of Siberia, and in the deserts of Asia and Africa, but I know of no silence so awe-inspiring, even terrible as that of a great pine forest." Evidently land like this did not bother Reed at all.

Shortly before 1799 he was able to buy 330 acres from the state of North Carolina at a price of fifty shillings per hundred acres, the going price at that time. There was nothing distinguished or especially talented about this immigrant. Everything about John Reed indicated that he was born to plow the hard red clay of Piedmont Carolina until he died, but that was not to be the case.

On a Sunday morning in 1799 John Reed had no thoughts beyond his family and his crops in his mind when he and his wife climbed upon his only horse to ride double to church. The distance was too far for the three children to walk, so the older son, Conrad, was placed in charge of the younger ones until their parents returned from services.

Twelve-year-old Conrad Reed took them down to Little Meadow Creek, which ran through the Reed farm, to shoot fish with a bow and arrow. While watching for fish, he

Twelve-year old Conrad Reed accidentally discovers a seventeen-pound gold nugget near Charlotte, North Carolina, in 1799.
(North Carolina Department of Archives and History Photo)   *Harper's New Monthly Magazine, 1857*

noticed a shiny yellow rock glinting in the sunlight and he waded in after it. It was far heavier to lift out than he had imagined; but he carried it back to the house and gave it to his father when he returned from church. It was about the shape of a small flatiron and just as heavy.

Reed had never seen such an unusual looking rock and he was sufficiently curious to take it to William Atkinson, a silversmith in the nearby village of Concord. The man who worked with silver did not recognize a more precious metal when he saw it and returned the rock to Reed telling him he had no idea what it could be. Back to his farm went Reed and for three years he used the seventeen-pound rock as a doorstop.

His crops flourished and in 1802 he was able to make a trip to Fayetteville over a hundred miles away, a trading center to the east on the Cape Fear River. Conrad who was going too, thought they should take their doorstop and his father humored him.

When they showed the rock to a Fayetteville jeweler, the man knew it for what it was and he had melted it down and showed John Reed a bar of gold six to eight inches long. Asked what he would sell it for, Reed who had no idea of the real value of gold replied with what he thought was a "big price."

"I will sell it for $3.50," he said and the jeweler immediately paid him. Reed was so happy to receive such a pile of money for "nothing" that he thought of pleasing his wife by bringing her something she had heard of but never seen or tasted . . . coffee.

Sarah Kizer Reed was at first pleased with the coffee but soon became exasperated when the unground beans did not cook up well when mixed with meat! Several weeks later word reached Cabarrus County through someone who had been down trading in Fayetteville that a jeweler there had sold a small bar of gold for "thousands of dollars." Reed saddled his horse and headed back to Fayetteville. There was a confrontation in the jewelry shop and John Reed returned home apparently bringing from one to four thousand dollars depending on which account is read. Possibly the jeweler parted with the money with the hope Reed would bring him more nuggets.

Reed had not thought of searching Little Meadow Creek for gold, but now he walked the creek and found that for a mile it was strewn with the precious metal.

For a time, farming was forgotten while each day the entire family went down to Little Meadow Creek to look for more rocks of gold. Some say the stream bed was covered with small golden nuggets shining beneath the surface and that Reed filled a quart jar with them. There was gold not only in the stream bed but in the gravel beside it where the Reeds found nuggets weighing up to twenty-eight pounds. John Reed was literally sitting on top of a gold mine for beneath the soil, the hills of his farm carried veins of milk white quartz and the precious metal.

It dawned on the former Hessian soldier that he was no longer in Europe where any gold discovered was automatically the property of the king but that the riches he was finding belonged solely to him. In Europe there had been no motivation for a gold rush for it must be turned over to the government. Here, a man had an opportunity to become rich overnight. Nearby farmers immediately began to dig on their own land. News of the Carolina gold rush was soon spreading throughout the southeast and the rest of the world!

John Reed expanded his operation taking in three farmer friends as partners and each summer after the crops were harvested, the partners supplied Reed with equipment and slaves to dig for gold in the creek bed and adjacent areas. The surface diggings near Little Meadow Creek were probably the richest in North Carolina. For the next twenty years, Reed and his partners continued seasonal mining operations along the creek and by 1824, their efforts had netted an estimated one hundred thousand dollars in gold.

In 1803 a nugget weighing twenty-eight pounds was found just under the surface of the ground by a gray-headed old slave named Peter and at the time, it was the largest nugget ever found in the United States. Thomas Hurley says in his book *Famous Gold Nuggets of the World* that this was the world's richest mining claim as to number, value and quality of the nuggets.

The half-mile of stream where the first nugget had been found was richer than any claim California would have almost fifty years later.

Although John Reed never learned to read and write, he became a wealthy man hiring servants and building a larger house of logs and stone. Other than that, his simple frugal lifestyle continued much the same.

Sadly enough, only four years after underground mining began in 1831, a family argument resulted in a court injunction that closed the mine for ten years. John Reed never saw it reopened for he died in 1845, but despite the closing of the mine he was still wealthy. After his death the Reed Mine was sold at public auction. Through the years the mine changed hands many times and mining was halted entirely at the Reed as well as throughout the state during the Civil War. The last large nuggett was found at the Reed by a placer miner in 1896 and a total was recorded of over one hundred pounds in gold nuggets before the last underground mining ceased in 1912.

As word spread, similar mining enterprises sprang up on the small farms that dotted the Yadkin and Catawba river valleys, including Parker's Mine in Montgomery County and Dunn's mine in Mecklenburg County. These "mines" were like the Reed partnership, really nothing more than placer operations along creek beds. Only after the most obvious large nuggets were discovered did these farmer-turned-miners began to use mechanical devices like the "rocker."

In 1828 a tired traveler spent the night with a shoemaker and his family at Brindletown in Burke County and the next morning saw flecks of gold in the clay chinking between the logs of the house. He borrowed a dishpan from the man's wife and panned more gold from the nearby stream than he had seen on all his travels in South America. Then he taught the shoemaker how to pan for gold and in return the shoemaker provided the land and the pair became partners. From that moment, the Burke County gold rush was on its way.

About forty-five miles above Raleigh, a man named Isaac Portis, who lived near two well traveled roads, took in lodgers for twenty-five cents a night. In 1838 he happened to take in a peddler bound from Raleigh to Halifax. As the peddler was leaving the next morning he became aware of the sun striking some glittering flecks in the freshly plowed red clay field. Filled with excitement, he hurried back to the house with a handful of earth. Samples of the earth sent to Raleigh and Richmond confirmed that Isaac Portis had been raising cotton in fields of gold. The northeast Carolina gold rush had begun.

Placer mining was replaced by vein mining in 1825 when it was discovered that underground veins of white quartz also bore gold. This "lode" gold as it was called required much more money, labor, and machinery. Fortune seekers from other countries were arriving and among them were skilled Cornishmen from England.

Entire families, even children from five or six years old up, worked in the mines. Gold mining at its peak employed more North Carolinians than any occupation other than farming but early census figures don't show this. Many of the men mined for gold when the crops were in but since they owned the land before the excitement over the discovery of gold, they saw themselves as "farmers" and this was what they put down as their occupation. Thus, census figures reflect only those working as employees at the larger mines, they don't count the scores of small one- or two-man claims nor do they count the farms where the owner and his slaves mined in the winter months.

HARD ROCK MINING BEGINS

The first recorded discovery of vein deposits of gold in the Carolina belt occurred in 1825 on the farm of Matthias Barringer. Like Reed, Barringer was a German farmer. He owned a few hundred acres of land in what is now Stanly County and he had panned for gold in the creeks on his farm for several years.

One day he noticed that beyond a certain point going up stream he could not find any gold. Just at the point where the gold seemed to stop, he saw a white quartz vein running into the hill and at right angles with the stream. He had often found pieces of the quartz with gold in it in the stream bed and he came to the conclusion that the gold scattered in the stream below this point must have come out of this particular quartz vein. He decided to pursue it into the hill.

He had followed it only a few feet when he struck a rich and beautiful deposit of the metal in a matrix of quartz. In following the vein for a distance of about thirty or forty feet and not more than fifteen or eighteen feet in depth, he found a succession of nests of gold from which he took out more than fifteen thousand pennyweights. There was great excitement in the area and within a few weeks fifty gold hunters had leased prospects from the old farmer.

What was most important to the North Carolina mining industry was that gold had been found in "regular veins."

Near Charlotte, several major mining properties developed including the Capp's Hill, McComb, and Rudisill mines. Now Piedmont farmers were leaving the streams and striking out for the hills and high ground. Meantime four or five shafts with depths up to ninety feet had opened up at the Reed Mine.

Throughout the Piedmont the pattern of vein discovery by farmers followed a similar one to that of Matthias Barringer. Using the most primitive machinery, the farmer mined the gold himself on a seasonal basis or leased his land to "gold hunters" for a percentage of the profits. Information concerning mining spread haphazardly by word-of-mouth and farmer-miners were on their own with little to guide them but intuition, trial and error, and some assistance from scientific texts or journals.

Robert W. Hodson, a Quaker from Guilford County, was typical of many of these farmer-miners of the 1820s. When he and his brother, Jeremiah, heard of a discovery of gold on a nearby farm they decided to do some prospecting on Jeremiah's land near Jamestown.

"From some knowledge of the geological strata of the earth," wrote Hodson in his journal ... "we coursed the vein over the high land to the next branch, thence upon the hill some distance, where a ledge of quartz jutted out, not more than a foot thick, leading south-southwest to the general course of ledges of rocks in the section of the country. We found some particles of gold in quartz."

But now was the season to plant crops and the brothers postponed their explorations until after summer's harvest, when they sank a pit about fifteen feet deep on the hill above the branch in search of gold. They found nothing. Robert Hodson was not dismayed by his failure and he spent the winter months absorbed in his studies of gold mining and milling.

"I applied my mind closely to gain a knowledge of Geology, Mineralogy and Metallurgy from the best books, papers and men, in my reach—the manner of gathering and working metals in Peru and elsewhere. Then we commenced work with a little better understanding of the manner of gathering gold in other countries by following the vein of quartz, washing the ore, grinding it and then applying mercury." They were able to save the pure gold but lost much of it that was mixed with other metals.

"When we succeeded in the work," Hodson wrote, "it produced wonderful excitement."

Men came from far and near, went to work sinking shafts at random and getting no pay. The Hodson Mine eventually reached a depth of fifty feet uncovering some valuable "pockets" of ore. The mine owners later employed a crew of three regular workers to dig, wash, and haul the ore. Usually, the men's wages varied from one dollar to thirty dollars a day.

In 1829 an unusual lady was touring the South making notes for a book on the region, as has been customary with northerners for years. Her name was Anne Newport Royal and one of the places she visited was the Hodson Brothers Mine. The mine was really a large open pit that had filled with water from rain and underground streams. They used no pumping equipment, only a primitive drain. Her description of mining which follows is very exact.

The ore is taken from the mine . . . in wheel barrows to a small creek where it is washed clean. It is then burnt and pulverized as it will not grind in its natural state. It is then removed into a wide box, made of plank, from two to three feet in length, about two feet wide. This box is open at the top to receive the ore and open at one end to let it run out.

The box is placed breast high from the ground, with the open end lower than the closed, while a trough like those which convey water to distilleries, passes immediately over the box. A hole through the trough lets the water fall upon the ore which is gradually washed into another trough. The water is raised into the trough overhead by a pump and this water issues in a small stream which nevertheless requires the aid of a hand to push the ore out into the next trough.

The second trough is of some length, perhaps ten or twelve feet. It also slopes more than the other. The water runs rapidly through this second box and spreads on the ground. This last box has notches cut in its bottom, perhaps an inch deep. Quicksilver is lodged in the notches and as the ore runs down over it, particles of gold stick to the quicksilver. The quicksilver is then taken out and laid on heated iron. It runs off leaving the gold which is then collected and run into bars in a furnace. This is the process!—simple enough.

The equipment and process resembled a combination of barrel rocker and long-tom that were used throughout the Piedmont. It was not a new procedure nor was it particularly complex. In fact it was used in Renaissance mines in Europe during the 1500s and in South America throughout the seventeenth and eighteenth centuries.

North Carolina farmers mined in a scientific vacuum piecing together bits of information from a variety of early sources. Mrs. Royal was direct in her criticism of their methods saying that there was "neither skill, machinery, capital, nor enterprise at the Hodson mine."

"Although the ore is . . . very rich and abundant . . . about two-thirds, to say the least, is wasted. In the first place, it is wasted in bringing it from the mines, in the wheel barrows;

Prospectors arrived from all over the United States and Europe.
Harper's New Monthly Magazine, 1857

then in the washing, and again in the burning, but most of all in the grinding. Instead of the furnaces, or kilns rather, it is thrown into common log-heaps, rain or shine, without shelter, and after it is burned, it is placed under a wheel which is pulled round . . . by a horse."

But instead of a box for the wheel to run in, and keeping it from wasting, the ore was on a few boards and with every turn of the wheel some of it would fall off on the ground. Here it was tramped into the earth and carried off on the miners' shoes. "A great part of it too, is lost, from not being ground fine enough. In short, it is wasted throughout the whole process, and the whole of the machinery is without shelter or system."

The machinery looks "as though it had been made by children with a penknife," said she, "poorly constructed and thoughtlessly deployed along the stream bed in a random fashion."

Of the miners themselves, she wrote, "It is laughable to see these tall, long-tail cotton-coat North Carolinians . . . poking about like snails, and picking up the quicksilver every now and then and eagerly squeezing it in their hands, to see how much gold is in it. They are so keen for the gold that they cannot wait till their day's work is done, which, the way they manage it, averages about 75 cents."

By leasing out small tracts of land to "poor people, who have neither skill nor capital to go on with the mining, and are averse to uniting with each other for their common benefit," the mine owners insure wasteful practices. Mrs. Royal's critical remarks were not unusual. Most observers of North Carolina's mining industry were struck by the poor training of the miners, the primitive nature of their equipment, and the wasteful methods used in milling the gold.

Dr. Richard Knapp of North Carolina's Division of Archives and History comments on the similar way the Reed Mine in Cabarrus County was operated saying, "For decades the Reeds ran their placer mine on an unscientific, inefficient basis primarily as a part-time family venture and this seeming lack of concern for increasing productivity typified much of the small but expanding Carolina mining industry."

In spite of their obvious shortcomings, men like John Reed, Matthias Barringer, and Robert Hodson laid the foundations of the North Carolina mining industry on their small family farms in the Piedmont in the 1820s and 1830s. It was crop rotation of a most unusual kind, the gold taking its turn at the proper season. Income from the gold also supplemented a farmer's income in years when crop prices were low.

A hundred and fifty years ago in North Carolina, all eyes were focused on a new and exciting newspaper published in Charlotte. It was the year 1830 and the paper was the *Miners and Farmers Journal* because practically every farm in the North Carolina Piedmont had a gold mine on it or at least a prospect. The newspaper was filled with ads for "gold mines" that were mostly deposit or placer mines located beside streams in scores of counties. Advertisements in the *Miners and Farmers Journal* emphasized the compatibility of mining and farming, although it was difficult enough to do one of these two occupations well without attempting both.

Of course, there had to be a nearer mint than Philadelphia. Farmers couldn't be making constant trips to take their gold to Philadelphia with the hazards of holdups along the way. In 1835, because of the pressure of southern representatives, Congress passed an act establishing branch mints in Charlotte; Dahlonega, Georgia; and New Orleans.

A farmer in Lincoln County wrote of his spring planting schedule in 1845, "I have planted 60 acres of corn, and I will not plant more until we have rain. I will keep some of the hands working a pretty fair gold vein on my land. I would not think of mining if it were not on my land, and we would have to let go our laborers or find new sources of income. I raised last year 27 bales of Cotton and got for it only something over $400. This is worse than flour at $3 per barrel. I am acting with caution in the gold business—Raising the ore first—not making the mill before we know what it will run on."

This was written twenty years after Hodson's account but it reflects the cautious attitude of North Carolina's farmer-miners. The mines were also a source of employment for unemployed farm laborers who wanted to find work near home.

By the 1830s much of the good farm land was no longer productive due to erosive farming methods and a mass emigration took place in which the more enterprising North

Carolinians went West for greater opportunity and greener fields.

Those that were left after the western exodus were not as venturesome nor did they have the technical "know how" and capital to turn the vast resources of the Carolina gold mines into efficient, scientific business operations.

In just a little more than ten years news of the California gold discovery was to race cross the country like wildfire; but the majority of these conservative North Carolina farmers were not the kind of men who would challenge hostile western Indians or brave Death Valley determined to make their fortunes.

Some political and economic leaders in the Piedmont recognized the geographic limitations of their region with its barren fields, poor access to trade, and the shortage of skilled labor. The federal government and the state of North Carolina were trying to provide a stable currency and to make incorporating easier.

The farm based society of the state was beginning to adopt, to a degree, a more receptive attitude toward the philosophy of work, money, and machinery. But it was foreign to the people of North Carolina and would be only a little less foreign to them a century later.

As North Carolina's mines evolved from placer to vein deposits, mine operators could no longer be part-time farmers. They were catapulted into the world of business, finance, and technology . . . ready or not. Raising capital sufficient to support the operations of a hard-rock gold mine required financial experience and techniques beyond that of a single owner or simple partnership. By granting incorporation charters to mining companies, the North Carolina General Assembly supported stock companies as a way to raise the large amounts of capital needed to purchase the machinery for hard-rock mines.

Men such as John M. Morehead, Archibald Murphey, William Graham, Charles Fisher, and others who saw the state's need for industrial development, were also early investors in mercantile businesses in the gold regions.

JOHN GLUYAS, A HARD-ROCK MAN

One of the greatest boosts North Carolina had to improve mining technology was the immigration of the Cornish. Some of the Cornish mines were the most modern and mechanized in the world and the fame of Cornish engineers was worldwide.

In 1795, just before Conrad Reed's discovery of gold in Little Meadow Creek, John Gluyas was born in the Parish of Wendron in Cornwall, England. He received his training as a civil engineer first in the depths of the copper and tin mines of his region and later in the mines and iron works of South Wales.

He began working in the late 1820s for William Brunton, a prominent engineer from London, and it was under Brunton's tutelage that Gluyas gained an impressive range of engineering skills. These skills were enumerated in the glowing letters of recommendation he carried with him to America.

"An Engineer of long standing, and of great eminence" he was commended for "superintending the laying down of a Railway, the formation of a long Inclined Plane, and the erection of a Steam Engine. Either as a Miner, a Mechanic, and as a superintendent of a Railway, we believe that he would be found a very useful, and valuable person to any party . . . Our opinion is so much in his favor that we would have gladly found him a situation had his determination not been irrevocably formed to try his fate in the New World."

The Cornishmen were skilled in hard-rock mining.
Harper's New Monthly Magazine, 1857

Why did a young man so respected in his profession in England take the drastic step of leaving his employment, his family and his homeland for an unknown country where he had no promise of employment when he arrived? Part of it was the frustrated ambition that he expresses in his letter to his brother.

I find that I must take the trouble and others have the profit. I intend to try something of my own next. I can be as well as I am now anytime. In considering our condition we have no home nor house. If I go on in this way and anything should happen to me our little money must go quickly and we have not got enough to buy something worth notice in this country for if there is a bit of land or anything of importance to be sold there is a plenty of Lawyers and Parsons and other lazy fellows who have money in Thousands brought to them by the labouring classes.

A labouring person have no honest chance in any way to do good for himself and family but to be a slave and rear his children in the same way. Since I find this to be the case I have determined to try some other Part of the world where I find others have gone and do a great deal better . . . in considering the whole it appears to me that the United States is by far the best (and in the same climate as we are in now) for a person who have a little money and understands the art of Manufacturing, of Minerals, Engineering, Farming, or . . . who will be industrious either as a Tradesman or Labourer.

No sooner had John Gluyas made his decision to leave England than he was faced not only with the disapproval of his family but the lure of "a confidential and permanent situation" in Wales. But Gluyas reasoned with himself, if I had not left Wendron, I would never have gotten more than forty shillings a month. I have been offered that in a week in Wales but in America I hope to get it in a day! He evaluated his abilities and observed that there was not one man in Cornwall who had the range of knowledge to instruct him in all the skills he had acquired. He had the courage to leave the familiar but oppressive behind him for the unknown in the hope that he would "have an honest chance" as he put it.

In August of 1834, John Gluyas with his wife and baby son, boarded a ship in Liverpool, and began the 52 day voyage. As it turned out later, Gluyas had left just in time, for an even more severe depression afflicted the mining industry of his mother country. He arrived at the port of New York in October with a small amount of money left, his letters of recommendation, and his drawings of engines and milling equipment. His first employment was in Mecklenburg County and he went on to supervise deep mining operations in Mecklenburg, Cabarrus, Davidson, and Montgomery counties in the 1830s and 1840s before arriving at Gold Hill in July of 1847.

These were the days when North Carolina was termed "the Golden State," and was leading in gold production until 1848 when the California gold rush began. An estimated value of the gold recovered in the state reached over a million dollars a year.

By 1850, it was said that half of the skilled miners at Gold Hill had been born in England, for the "hungry forties" as they were called created a new wave of migration due as much to the potato blight in Europe as to opportunities in the New World. Like the men who came before them, the Cornish miners of the 1840s migrated as families and upon their arrival entered into partnership with local farmers and native gold hunters.

John Gluyas had formed a partnership with another Cornishman, William Treloar, and leased a lot from David Troutman along the Rowan and Cabarrus County line promising to pay Troutman 10 percent of their total profits. They installed two Chilean mills to grind the ore, one horse-powered, the other driven by steam, possibly the first steam powered mill in the Gold Hill district. Gluyas left the daily management of the milling operation there to his partner and was busily engaged with the development and management of several other mining locations in the Piedmont including mines in Montgomery and Guilford counties. This enterprising Cornish engineer retired to Asheboro where he died in 1858.

Three years later the Civil War brought North Carolina gold production to an abrupt halt. On Saturday morning, April 20, 1861, Confederate forces under the command of Colonel J. Y. Bryce, seized the mint at Charlotte and the gold coins. The three federal employees in the building did not resist and for four years the building was a Confederate military headquarters.

The only mine in Charlotte to survive the war was the Rudisil, operated by J. H. Carson, whose ingenuity and perseverance managed to keep the mine going while others had to close. Many Charlotteans were able to endure the devastation of the Reconstruction days only because of the treasure from the Rudisil Mine three hundred feet beneath the ground. The Civil War dealt a staggering blow to the already declining Carolina gold mines, but by this time gold had been found and produced in more than half of North Carolina's one hundred counties.

The Reed Gold Mine now belongs to the State of North Carolina and is estimated to have produced over ten million dollars in gold. It is the site of the first authenticated gold find in the United States, the discovery which touched off the nation's first gold rush. The mine has been designated a National Historic Landmark.

Throughout the 1830s and 1840s, gold miners carried their picks across both Carolinas, down into Georgia and Alabama and many became part of a great western migration of both miners and settlers.

2.
The Specter of the Reed Mine

Our story begins in the early 1800s with a miner named William Mills, a good man and a sound man ... an Englishman by birth whose home was Wales. Like many other men who left Western Europe to seek riches during the Carolina gold rush, Mills had settled among a group of miners in the shacks and tents surrounding a boom town.

It was December and the winter's first snow storm blurred the outlines of the shanties. Walking home from the mine, Mills congratulated himself that he had gone to Georgeville the day before and put in a good supply of victuals. Even if it were not for the saloons and drunkenness, the shootings were enough to keep any decent, sensible fellow away from the town after dark.

He had also split over a cord of wood for the fire and he looked forward to it, what with the penetrating wind and the snow. Not that he always found the home fires burning when he came from the mine. Many times he would come in to a cold house with the fire out and his wife, Eleanor, lying on the cornshuck mattress beneath a pile of soiled quilts.

How he wished he had never brought her to North Carolina from England, for day after day he heard nothing but complaints. At night her voice kept him awake talking of Liverpool and her friends there ... demanding shrilly that he take her back.

This afternoon he was returning home after a day of backbreaking labor digging out the red clay and then working down one pan after another in the icy stream ... but his tiredness was unimportant so elated was he over finding the largest nuggets he had yet seen on his claim. He could scarcely wait to show them to her and see the pleasure on her face. Yes, they would go back but only when he could return a rich man. Today's find brought them a step closer to England. Never again would he work as a millwright; he would take the vials of gold dust he had panned with such patience and his nuggets and buy a small business of his own. People would work for *him*.

When he entered the cabin, Eleanor scarcely spoke to him busying herself at the fireplace with the cook pots. He could hear her muttering something about Liverpool and he hoped this was not the beginning of one of her harangues.

The winter wind had begun to howl fiercely, tearing at the small log house. Eleanor bent over the fireplace and pushed the iron pot on its trivet closer to the flames. As she poked the logs with a large hickory stick, eerie shadows moved grotesquely on the walls. The only light in the room came from the fire and two small oil lamps, each with a twisted, tallow-soaked rag which burned dimly and emitted a greasy, black smoke.

"And this is what I have come to from a comfortable, happy home in Liverpool where I was loved and cherished," Eleanor whined. Her blonde hair hung in wisps about her face, damp, snakelike tendrils moistened by the puffs of steam from the pot.

"I have eaten squirrel, rabbit, possum, every sort of wild varmint you bring into this house. My, aren't you proud of them? And, when have I last had a taste of something decent like mutton? I ask you?" Mills did not reply.

"What a God forsaken wilderness this place is."

The heavyset man with his head of full, black curly hair and thick brown beard sat down at the table. A rough table he had made with his own hands. He reached into his shirt pocket, pulled out a leather pouch and spilled its contents on the table. There was the sound of metal on wood as gold nuggets rolled across it. He looked toward Eleanor for some reaction but she appeared to scarcely notice them.

"Eleanor, Eleanor, look what I have here. Aren't you . . ."

"How long are we going to stay? You certainly lied to get me to come to this uncivilized Carolina, promising me silk and satin and gold rings for my fingers."

"But you'll have them. You'll have them yet!" She burst into wild, mocking laughter.

"What a husband you turned out to be, and to think I was once a fine lady's maid." The man at the table did not try to answer her again nor did he look up.

"Say something! Answer me you miserable wretch. You have become just like the rest of the louts around here. How filthy you are! I wonder how a woman like myself ever married the likes of you!"

William Mills looked his wife full in the face for the first time and tiny flames ignited in his blue eyes. He was a temperate man but her continual nagging drove him almost out of his mind. Without answering, he went on examining the nuggets on the table.

"You never listen to me!" she shouted, and her hand suddenly shot out sweeping his precious nuggets all over the floor. A wave of rage surged through him and he could feel his face grow flaming hot as if suffused with liquid fire. He rose and started toward her but at that moment came the sound of a bang. One of the shutters had been wrenched open by the wind. He managed to tie it securely with a leather thong and went back into the house.

By then he had calmed down some and he began picking up the nuggets on the floor. He sat back down at the table to wait on his supper. He couldn't trust himself to say anything to her for if he had, he knew it would produce another avalanche of abuse. Finally, she brought him a bowl filled with the most evil smelling concoction imaginable and stood beside him glaring and holding the bowl.

He moved the nuggets to one side and as he did Eleanor slammed the bowl on the oak table with such ferocity that the soup slopped over the edge of the earthenware bowl and scalded his right hand. The weather had been so cold and his hands had suffered so much from exposure that the skin on the back of his knuckles was a mass of raw cracks and the pain from the salty, almost boiling soup was nearly unbearable. It took every bit of control he possessed not to get up and violently shake the creature who now seated herself sullenly across from him.

Lord! He felt guilty for the way he had come to hate her. Eleanor had pressed him to marry her, then begged to be taken along when he told her that their Cornish and Welsh friends were leaving to make a fortune in Carolina. A few short weeks after their arrival she had begun to make his life miserable.

Tonight, she was dressed in one of the elaborate gowns from her trunk at the foot of the bed. There she sat in these primitive surroundings bedecked with lace and silk. But the dress was covered with food spots and the lace bedraggled. Eleanor Mills' face wore a savage, sarcastic expression as she presided with mock courtesy over the unsavory liquid in the soup tureen.

"And, may I help you to more of this delicious soup, Mr. Mills?"

She half rose as if to refill his bowl. As he started to say no, he heard the sound of ripping silk. Eleanor had stepped on the hem of her dress, lost her balance and was falling. Her head struck the corner of the oak slab that served them for a bench and down she went in a heap on the clay floor. The silk dress surrounded her like the dirty pink petals of a crumpled rose, her head rested in the center, facedown upon the folds.

He lifted her chin with a finger and saw a deep, triangular gash across her forehead. A rivulet of blood ran down from it and began to stain the lace around her throat. Perhaps she had only fainted. He bathed her face in cold water but there was no response. The warmth of the fire would revive her he thought. He wrapped her in a blanket, pulled the mattress closer to the fire and, lifting her upon it, lay down at her side and fell asleep.

Sometime in the early part of the night he awakened to find the room cold and noticing that the fire had died down he replenished the logs. He was almost asleep when he heard a spectral voice say, "Oh, William. I'm so tired of all this. You must take me home right away." He turned over and stared into her face. But it was too dark to see her well so he got up and lit a candle. Her mouth sagged open and her lips had turned blue. Eleanor Mills was dead.

Perspiration broke out upon his forehead. Surely the voice he had just heard had only been his imagination. It had all been an accident and in the morning he would do whatever was needed to see that she got a decent burial. Then a disturbing thought occurred to him. There were some who knew that he and his wife quarreled. Would they think he had killed her? His heart beat fast as he considered the possibility that people would accuse him of murder!

Somehow, he must get rid of Eleanor's body. First he would get some branches, tie them together and make a litter for the body. His hand was on the door latch to go outdoors when he again heard the voice and this time it cried out more loudly, "William! If you don't take me home, I will have to stay here in this cabin with you forever."

Large, muscular man that he was, Bill Mills began to tremble all over with fear. Seizing another blanket from the bed he wrapped it around his wife's limp body. He was now determined to get her out of the cabin. Carrying the blanketed form which was heavier than he had ever imagined Eleanor to be, the tall, dark figure set out in a driving snowstorm toward the Reed Mine.

Sometimes his feet slipped beneath him and once he dropped her in the snow as he made his way slowly up the hill of the Reed. Finally, he reached the top. Not far away was the Engine Shaft, one of the deepest vertical tunnels, but now abandoned. He would drop the body into the depths and there it would never be discovered. When he reached the shaft, he unwrapped the blankets and hoisted the corpse over the edge.

Great God in heaven! Was that a cry he heard coming up toward him from the shaft below or was it the wind wailing? His hands almost frozen, his beard stiff with snow, he stumbled down the thickly forested hill avoiding the placer pits and back to his cabin.

Because of the snowstorm, it was two days before the men were able to go back to work and over a week before anyone noticed they had not seen Eleanor Mills recently. When they asked her husband about her, he replied that she was feeling puny and had taken to her bed. A week later he announced that she had thought it would do her good to go to Charleston and visit relatives newly arrived from Liverpool. For several weeks he lived alone quite peacefully. Until one night he was awakened by the piercing wail of a woman's voice.

"William, oh, William! What have you done to me? It's so horribly cold and dark down here...." And night after night this went on until there was no longer any sleep for William Mills. He soon began drinking heavily at the local bars.

And when did the first whispers begin? No one really knows, only that there was talk. Until a peddler arriving with a full wagon of wares for the miners left hurriedly one morning. He said he had camped near the Engine Shaft the night before and heard the terrified shrieks of a woman calling "William! William!" Shortly afterward Mills disappeared from the Georgeville area. Some thought he was on his way to the new diggings at Dahlonega, Georgia. Others said it was because he knew more of his wife's disappearance than he cared to admit. In any event, he was never seen again.

Years later when the echo of picks in the hard, milk white quartz of Cabarrus County had faded away, the woods around the Engine Shaft were cut down for timber. But the men made certain they left before dusk for they had heard the terrifying shrieks near the Engine Shaft at night.

This story is told by the great-grandson of one of the miners who claims that the tormented Mills confided his story after his tongue was loosened by drink. And that he left for Georgia convinced his wife's spirit would haunt him as long as he stayed on at the Reed.

If the bones of Eleanor Mills should someday be brought up and returned to England, would the screams of the specter of the Engine Shaft forever be stilled? Now, tourists trample the wild flowers that grow on the large hill above the Reed Mine Museum, and small creatures scurry below in the darkness of the old shafts. And even though the Reed is a historic site, there are few who would care to spend a night alone near the Engine Shaft.

For the wind that rattles the branches of the oaks and hickory trees cannot always drown out the sound of a woman's screams and a voice that even now may be crying, "It's so cold, it's so dark down here . . . William, William, help me get out!"

3.

The Legendary Walter George

Let us pretend that by some time warp, it *is* one hundred years ago. We are in the village of Gold Hill, base of operations for Walter George Newman, one of the most colorful characters of the North Carolina gold rush; and everywhere we look are superstructures of mine shafts, huge piles of ore and the vast machinery of stamp mills.

And there on Main Street is Walter George himself! Today, he is dressed like a city financier, but a touch more flamboyantly, in his dark suit with an ascot at his throat. As he hurries down the street on his way to the mine, Newman is a marked contrast to his surroundings where storefronts have the look of the Old West and horse drawn wagons are pulled up in front of them.

Rough looking bearded men with heavy boots lift their hats to him as they swagger down the unpaved, muddy Main Street. Along with the pungent odor of wood smoke in the cold winter air is the indefinable smell of gold . . . an atmosphere of underlying excitement . . . of something always just about to happen. Walter George is going to be sure that it does, for his pockets are crammed with gold nuggets and one contains a vial filled with gold dust.

A lovely young woman sits waiting in a fashionable carriage while the villagers of Gold Hill mining community pass and stare, curious to get a glimpse of Mrs. Walter George Newman. Inside the gleaming, black stanhope, she looks at her diamond and sapphire watch impatiently, recrosses her legs and for a moment there is a glimpse of black silk hose. It is almost time for the private train from New

36

York to arrive with their important guests. But where is Walter George?

He said he had to make a trip to the mine. Why did he want to go over there like this at the last minute? He will be back though, even if the train is pulling in as he arrives. And at that moment a plump, pink faced man in a derby hat appears and jumps in beside her. We are here in time to catch a typical Walter George Newman production.

Mrs. Newman looked at her husband as he got in the carriage. His face was perspiring and there was dirt on the sleeve of his almost ostentatiously expensive suit, but he was grinning like a boy. She wiped his forehead and then flicked his sleeve with her handkerchief.

"Is something funny?"

"My dear, that is going to be the richest mine our guests have ever seen. They will be literally stumbling over the gold."

"George, you haven't . . ."

"Oh, but I have. Now, don't pretend to be so innocent. What do you think buys these?" He reached over and lifted the edge of her skirt exposing a silk clad ankle. "And baubles like this?" He touched her diamond watch. "Would they buy company stock the way they do if I showed them a mine with no gold?"

The whistle of a train was heard and here it came, the small steam engine emitting clouds of steam into the crisp winter air pulling behind it a burgundy red Pullman car. "The Gold Hill Consolidated Company" embellished the side of the Pullman in brilliant gold letters. A red carpeted platform was pulled into place for the passengers to step upon, and a uniformed black porter took each visitor's arm as a dozen affluent businessmen emerged.

Richly attired in dark suits and overcoats, gold watch chains glittering across their middle, some had a copy of the *Wall Street Journal* under their arm and all carried expensive valises. In a moment an expansive, cordial Walter George was in their midst, the center of attention. He introduced his wife and for a few minutes the group stood exchanging pleasantries.

Of course, the Wall Streeters were impressed by Walter George's private Pullman, for here was a man of extravagant tastes surrounded with the most glittering trappings of success. The Newman "treatment" of potential investors included the train that had transported them here, replete with a bar and, on this occasion, an entire New York floor show for their entertainment.

"Refreshments! First refreshments!" he said motioning with a grandiose gesture in the direction of the Newman mansion and the men followed Walter George and his beautiful wife. Inside there was food and the sound of corks popping as bottles of imported champagne were opened and poured. It was almost two hours before the party reappeared on the porch of the house, and with Gold Hill's impressed citizens gaping, the visitors from New York were transported to the mine in two elegant tallyho carriages each drawn by a team of shining black horses.

Walter George led the way. Everywhere there was activity and men hard at work. The miners scarcely looked up except for a foreman here and there who would nod respectfully to Mr. Newman. Suddenly, Newman stopped and the group behind him came to a standstill. In his colorful way, he had been confiding in them boasting of the incredible amounts of ore shipped and all the gold this mine was producing. Now he casually pointed out flecks of gold on the ground near an ore bucket. They were impressed.

"Gentleman, you cannot imagine how rich the ore of this mine is. I have seen veins just like this one laden with gold." He brushed the edge of a streak of the milky quartz with his finger, lightly, and carelessly, then looked where he had just touched the wall of the tunnel and exclaimed dramatically, "My God! Look what we've discovered."

"Why, it's a regular nest of nuggets!" He thrust his palm out dramatically and excited visitors crowded around him. As they left the mine who should walk up but his brother, Joe. One of the men immediately told him about the nuggets Walter George was holding in his hand and his brother asked to see them. Joe started to laugh for he suspected Walter George of seeding the mine before the visitors arrived but when he saw the anger flare in his brother's eyes he fell silent.

Now, Walter George led the way to his office where, amid great pomp, he unlocked the guarded safe and withdrew something wrapped in black velvet and covered with gold dust. He threw back a corner of the cloth and brought into full view a nugget of amazing size. There were great gasps and exclamations from the financiers, and all the while Newman sat back smoking his big cigar, allowing others to talk and slowly but surely closing the trap around them.

"What did Mr. Newman think the mine needed in the way of machinery? Was he able to hire as many workers as he thought he would need? Could he build concentrating plants right here at Gold Hill instead of shipping the ore off?"

Walter George nodded, agreed that more money was needed to do these things and then, could scarcely accept their checks fast enough. Meanwhile, Joe Newman, stood off to one side and watched his brother with contempt. Soon the visitors were admiring the elaborate cartouche of miners at work in the center of the impressive Gold Hill Consolidated Company stock certificates and stashing away hundreds of stock shares in their valises. Before the trail pulled out, Walter George had "fleeced the wolves of Wall Street."

Walter George Newman was born in Orange County, Virginia, in 1860. Little is known of his youth save that he claimed to have worked as a stable boy for Governor Roswell Flowers. He always had style and was usually seen sporting a derby hat, a scarf at the throat and carrying a black silk umbrella. In later life the scarf was secured by a pin made from a large gold nugget "as big as a hen's egg." In his watch pocket he carried a solid gold watch and the men around the mining camp said that in its case was the sort of picture that hung behind many a Western bar.

He drove one of the finest teams of black horses in Rowan County and their fancy harness was attached sometimes to a stanhope, sometimes to a tallyho carriage. As soon as he arrived, Walter George began the mansion across the road from the mining office and not until it was completed did his beautiful wife join him in Gold Hill.

Mrs. Newman often went riding in a fine carriage driven by a handsome groom and once when she was gone for a long time, gossip had it that Mrs. Newman had ridden out one day with the handsome groom and would not be back . . . this, despite her husband's thoughtfulness in hiring two black boys to run along before the carriage to throw any rocks to one side that might cause discomfort. Whether it was truth or talk, no one really knew, but she did return.

First to own an automobile in Gold Hill, Walter George was so proud of it that he had a picture of it etched on the back of a thin, gold pocket watch that he gave an employee friend.

Another employee's daughter said, "We also have the remnants of two sets of dishes that Mr. Newman gave us quite unexpectedly, following his threats to dynamite our house, and I think my parents were worried at the time because he was so unpredictable no one ever really knew what he would do." There was no doubt that he could be a violent man and no one was safe from his anger.

As Newman himself said, he first heard about the riches of the Gold Hill district from his brother Joseph J., a mining engineer who had worked in the North Carolina mines since the early 1880s. It was soon apparent to all that Walter George's greed knew no limits, for he tried to buy out his brother but his offer was not accepted. The pair were in a local tavern one night when Walter George, in a particularly ugly mood, began shouting vicious accusations and calling Joseph names. Familiar with Walter George's tantrums, men began to slink out of the tavern one by one.

A few weeks later all of Gold Hill was awakened in the middle of the night by an earthshaking explosion. Joseph Newman and his modest home had been destroyed. Investigation showed that a charge of dynamite had exploded under Joseph's bed as he slept. "Suicide," said Walter George who was his sole heir and would now inherit the property he had been trying his best to purchase. A charge of dynamite under the bed was a singular way to commit suicide and many suspected Walter George of murder although none dared accuse him.

In the final months of 1898, Newman began to buy tracts of mining properties along the Rowan and Cabarrus county line and in a year's time he owned the Union Mining Company holdings, the old Honeycutt Gold Mine, the Earnhardt, the Heilig and the Randolph Shafts—the major mining properties of Gold Hill. He still had admirers.

A prospectus and stock certificate from the Gold Hill mines donated by
the notorious Walter George Newman.
(Photo by Bruce Roberts)

"He has set two blades of grass growing where only one
grew before," praised a newspaper writer. A bustling mining town blossomed under Newman's direction confirming
everyone's optimism. In a burst of beneficence, he had a
Children's Park constructed at Gold Hill. Since company
records show children as young as five years old worked in
the mines, the park was probably not used by many of them.

Yet another story of this unfathomable man involved a
sick child and a mother in distress. Newman passed the pair
in his coach but thinking it over he turned the carriage
about, hurried back and after inquiring the woman's mis-

sion immediately put her and the child in the seat. He told her to hasten to town and that he would be there if she needed money. The grateful woman drove off in his carriage and Newman set off toward the village on foot in his linen duster and derby hat. The farther he walked, the hotter he grew and the hotter he grew the more clothes he shed.

Soon he began to feel as though he were literally burning up and off came his trousers and shirt. When he finally finished the three-mile stretch and arrived at the mine office in Salisbury, he shocked his employees by appearing only in his derby hat, underwear, shoes and socks. But they were probably used to the cruder side of his nature for he sponsored cockfights, repugnant to most people, and claimed that he was a champion spitter! Only in the rough isolation of a mining community could a Walter George Newman have flourished and inspired the loyalty of the men.

He undoubtedly had a wild and violent streak, for one night he convened a "battle royal" of black workers on the platform of Gold Hill's railroad station. It was a fight to the finish for the pot of gold announced by Newman—and what a brawl!

It was a grand melee with every man for himself. All the while Newman was yelling, leaping, snorting, and shouting with joy. The ultimate winner was knocked out in the beginning and played possum until near the end when the last two fighters were walking around in a daze . . . then he got up and finished off the two tired and battered survivors. Viewing the spectacle from his vantage point on the balcony, Walter George strutted back and forth, encouraging first one fighter and then his opponent.

As the new century of 1900 began, this man single-handedly breathed life into the moribund mining industry of Gold Hill where copper, not gold was now the source of employment.

The plant was processing over one hundred and fifty tons of ore daily and shipping about fifty carloads of thirty thousand pounds each to concentrating plants in New Jersey. Meanwhile five huge concentrating plants were under construction at Gold Hill representing, "the greatest activity ever witnessed in a mining camp in this State," according to a correspondent for the *Engineering and Mining Journal*.

To support his venture, Newman secured the backing of some Boston businessmen and by September 1899, the Union Copper Mining Company had transformed its property at Gold Hill. They constructed all new facilities and dwellings to accommodate a work force of one thousand men. In August of 1900, Walter George with his straight, sandy-colored hair parted in the middle and combed flat and a satisfied look on his plump face strode confidently among the boilers, pumps, and drills all busily at work. He was in his glory.

That summer the rotund figure in the wrinkled white suit was often seen standing on the porch of the big, two-piece office building on the hill tugging on his reddish mustache and staring out proudly over a large and prosperous mining enterprise. But he had operated all of this for less than a year when a cash shortage suddenly forced him to turn the mine over to managers from Colorado. Within a year's time he had managed to direct two companies into failure.

By installing a new concentrator, the Colorado interests made the mine more efficient and for the next three years it produced rich copper ore but soon the mine was again in the throes of serious financial problems. The years between 1900 and 1910 were tumultuous, for the mines were run alternately by the receivership, the western directors of the company, and Newman.

Ownership of the Gold Hill mines resembled a closely contested prize fight and those who followed it with deep interest must have been saying to each other, "He's up, no, he's down. He's up again!" At intervals, Walter George Newman would step melodramatically back on center stage to follow his usual pattern of extravagant promises, a huge investment of money, and little or no return in either gold or copper.

As the mine shafts at Gold Hill proliferated so did Walter George Newman's problems with his stockholders and company officers. The following angry letter berating his company treasurer in New York rests in the files of the *Salisbury Post*.

Dear Sir:

How you can take the truth and misconstrue it into an insult is beyond me. You are not worth the time it takes to insult you. You have never been any help to me. You were put in as treasurer to help Phillips unload on me the stock of the Gold Hill Consolidated Co. He is no longer a stock holder hence your insulting remarks to a man who has brought a sunken ship safely into port. As for the board of directors in the past, what have they done in the past seven years but loot the treasury, and stand in the way of any advancement ... I have no time to argue with you and it's beneath my dignity to argue with a hireling.

In your present capacity, I take notice that you used up four hundred and thirty-five dollars of the money and paid it out without any knowledge of mine ... and because I need the money here to pay the men . . . you set up a howl and have a cloven hoof. So, I would advise you to prevent any further trouble that you do as directed by wire today. I have not lost my grip yet, and I will show you who has the authority to do the right thing and see that it is done.

Very respectfully,
Walter George Newman, President

Reenter Walter George Newman serving as president in 1909. He immediately put one hundred men to work but by September he had failed and the mine was sold in a fore-closure proceeding. Determined to succeed, Newman did not let go and in order to raise more money to reopen the mines, after he had exhausted his sources on Wall Street, he turned to friendly senators in Washington even having the gall to use Senate Committee stationery. This led to an investigation that incurred some of the New York press's most sarcastic remarks.

Walter George spent his final months in Gold Hill strug-gling to keep his mine running and pay his employees; but the public exposure of the Senate hearing had hurt his credibility for securing long-term financial backing and the people of Gold Hill knew him too well.

Many honest men had toiled to make these mines pay. The real geological problem appears to have been that the gold was in small flecks and so difficult to separate from other metals that much of it was lost. One mining authority familiar with Gold Hill properties estimated six million dollars in pure gold was actually shipped out of Gold Hill but seventy-two million washed down the Yadkin River never to be recovered.

Walter George's last exploit at Gold Hill was a bedraggled replay of earlier ones. He arrived there just ahead of yet another carload of potential investors from New York, but company finances were at such a low point that this time the Northerners had to pay their own way down. Newman now borrowed money from the unemployed miners to buy paint and whitewash. Quickly rounding up workers he hired them to paint the buildings at the Gold Hill Mine ... then hustled them out of their overalls and into miner's outfits just in time for the financiers on tour to see them hard at work down in the shafts. A master con artist to the last, his game worked again and investors eagerly contributed twelve thousand dollars to help him develop the mine further.

After the visitors left, angry, shouting miners who in addition to the money for the paint were also owed back wages, converged on the office building cornering Newman on the second floor balcony. He promised, he cajoled, and he attempted to pacify the crowd without success. Suddenly he astonished everyone by raising both arms above his head and showering dollar bills and coins from the balcony into the crowd below. In the confusion that followed, Newman slipped out the back door, boarded his private train and sped off while the miners scrambled for what turned out to be Gold Hill's last payroll.

A mythical quality surrounded this man and even by the end of his days at Gold Hill the exact truth and chronology of all the stories about him no longer seemed to matter. After he drifted away from the area, he separated from his wife and apparently wandered throughout the country for some time before he was heard of again back in New York.

There, alone in his hotel suite, he died at the very moment his wife was obtaining her divorce. Newman was fifty-eight years old and the year was 1918. He was still wearing an ascot at his throat when he was found but the large gold nugget pin was gone.

Miners and their families, big money investors from the northeast, everything in Gold Hill existed in the shadow of his towering presence. Only the deafening roar of ore being crushed by the monstrous iron stamp mills created as lasting an impression of the town as did Walter George Newman—shrewd, spectacular, mysterious, violent.

Newman stood out, not for his financial genius, not even for his rascality but because he was a figure of gargantuan proportions ... a folk hero and a folk villain of whom the most extravagant story could be true. Whenever the North Carolina gold rush is recalled, there will always be stories of a village called Gold Hill ... and the legendary Walter George.

4.

The Grisly Ghost of Gold Hill

Does the violent, rowdy past sometimes stir and come alive in the isolated little village of Gold Hill? Some say the past does not rest easy in this once glittering boom town of North Carolina's gold rush days. The experience this story is based upon took place on a January night in 1954.

Clouds scuttered restlessly across the face of the moon, its light now and then revealing the dark gallows of old beams stretching skyward above the long-abandoned Randolph Mine. And not far from the mine the rustling leaves of a giant oak masked the whispers of two shadowy figures.

Carol Eisenhower and John Earnhardt had rendezvoused here before, the low limbs of the post oak's tenacious leaves clinging long after other trees were bare, concealing the young lovers. Almost every evening, they found excuses to leave their parents' homes after dark. Tonight an hour had swiftly passed and their good-byes as always were reluctant.

Suddenly, the frightened voice of a woman rang out as clearly as if she stood beside them.

"Good Lord! What will happen to me? I am sure he suspects and he may very well kill me."

"He wouldn't dare," a man's voice replied. "He's never really tried to harm you has he?"

Carol and John listened, too shocked to move.

"Not yet, Roger, but his rages terrify me . . . and after what he has done. . . ."

"What do you mean? What *has* he done?"

"You must be the only one in Gold Hill who doesn't know. Everyone else does even though no one will say a word openly. He inspects the mines, he sits in his office, he stops off at the bars."

"What has Walter George done?"

"Haven't you seen how the men stare at him . . . then they look down and fiddle with their glass or they turn their head away so their eyes won't meet his."

"Come out with it!"

"The miserable cowards don't dare accuse him openly because of that vicious temper of his . . . *but they know* . . . and don't think he has fooled me, his own wife."

"Marie! What are you talking about!"

"Call him Cain! Don't call him Walter George for he has murdered his own brother."

"*Murdered Joe?*"

"Blown Joe Newman to bits . . . that's what he's done and while the poor man slept innocent in his bed."

"My God! How can you say that, Marie. He wouldn't go that far."

"He wouldn't? He would do anything for money, you poor fool. That man is the Devil himself."

"You worry because you think he knows about us."

Perhaps, he does and if he has his way, Roger, something just as bad will happen to you and to me!"

"Marie . . . don't get so upset. Even if you are right, I won't let him harm you," and then a piercing scream rent the air. Carol and John stood petrified, unable to imagine what was happening.

"Look! Over there to your left. Do you see something floating in the air? Something like the pieces of a body?" The woman's voice trembled.

"Good Lord!"

"It's Joe Newman!"

"Great heavens . . . is that a face?"

"Yes. O-o-h!"

"Do you see the eyes? They are coming right toward us."

John could feel Carol trembling and they were both too frightened to make a sound.

"I can't bear the sight of those eyes!" they heard the woman cry out.

And then the deep, terrifying exclamation of a man, "Gawd!"

A woman's scream trailed off into hysterical sobs and as John and Carol gazed into the darkness they saw a most hideous sight. The parts of a human body floated toward them in midair, each limb was clearly recognizable but with a weird, luminous appearance. As if in slow motion, a man's arm drifted by . . . so close they thought the clawing fingers might touch them . . . now a foot could be seen but with no leg. Then, shocking to behold, a ghostly head began to approach bobbing crazily through the air.

The young couple shrank back against the oak and watched in horror.

On came the monstrous, tumescent head, eyes rolling wildly, until it was scarce an arm's length away. Carol shut her eyes, feeling faint. When she finally dared open them the head was a fading, blurry blob and the conversation was still going on.

"He will be back from New York tomorrow. Roger, let's leave in the carriage tonight or it may be too late," she pleaded. This was followed by the sharp crack of a whip, the frightened whinny of horses and the sound of what could only have been a carriage nearby hurtling along at a wild pace, its wheels creaking and rattling.

"Hurry, Roger, before someone at the mining company sees his carriage and tries to stop us." There was a rush of wind so close to them and so strong that the leaves from the ground rustled, rose, and swirled up into their faces. The boy and girl stood terrified waiting to be run down . . . then the sounds of the carriage faded away into the night. Carol was trembling.

"I've never been so frightened. What was all that?"

"I'm not sure I know. At least I don't know why we were the ones to see such a horrible thing! Carol, have you heard the stories about the days when this was a boomtown and the gold mines were going strong?"

"The old men are always talking about those days . . . but who were the couple we heard talking and how can you explain such a horrible sight?"

"I can't entirely . . . but you do know that a man named Walter George Newman was once the wealthiest mine owner in this area?"

"I've heard his name many times."

"Walter George and his brother had a violent argument and almost came to blows. It was at one of the taverns and a great many of the miners heard it. Together the brothers owned one of the richest mines in Rowan County and Walter wanted Joe to sell out. When his brother refused, Walter George was furious with him."

"But lots of families have arguments."

"Carol, do you know what kind of man Walter George was? He was hot-headed, ruthless . . . his business scandals made news headlines."

"That doesn't mean he would murder someone though does it?"

"I think he would have done anything. A few nights after their quarrel there was a terrible explosion and everyone went running out of their houses to see what had happened. They found one entire side of Joe Newman's house laid open where it had exploded and he had been blown to bits

... killed by a charge of dynamite that went off under his bed while he was asleep. Everyone thought Walter George did it to make himself sole owner of the mine."

"And the couple we heard talking?"

"Not long after his brother's death Newman came back from one of his trips to New York to find his wife gone and he went out to look for her."

"Then she and that man really did go off together?"

"I heard she ran away with the driver of one of his finest carriages and took it with them. They say she was beautiful and loved luxury and that because of that carriage Newman found them. No one knows what became of the coachman but Newman brought her back claiming that she had been kidnapped."

"Do you think we really heard his wife ... or rather her ghost?"

"I don't know, Carol, but as that carriage went past I believe a stone thrown out by one of the wheels hit my leg," and the boy put his hand down and grimaced as he touched his shin. His fingers felt something sticky and when he held them up to the light there was a wet, crimson stain upon them.

Years later, long after Carol Eisenhower had become Carol Earnhardt, she and John would sit by the fireside and tell their children a story. A story of how their father had received the scar on his leg and the horror of the time the dead came back to haunt a forgotten village called Gold Hill.

On January nights near the old Randolph shaft the leaves of the giant oak still rustle in the winter wind; and sometimes there are those who say they have heard carriage wheels, raised voices, and a woman's scream.

Are ghosts real and is there any such thing as a ghost carriage? Is it possible that at the right time and in the right

place past events are still capable of regenerating themselves, unleashing a weird and fearsome sort energy? John
Earnhardt looks at the scar where the stone struck his leg
and he is tempted to answer—yes!

An old-time prospector says the specter of Walter George
still stalks the streets of this village in the soft gray light of
early morning, strides confidently toward the site of his
office, emerges at dusk from a shaft of his richest mine. For
only Gold Hill, the place where Newman came so close to
making a fortune, could draw this peculiar man back again
and again. From John and Carol's experience it would seem
that there are times when Walter George's wife and
coachman are there too ... along with his not quite "all
together" brother, Joe.

Greeting Joe must be quite a shock even for Walter
George.

5.
The Discovery of
Gold in Virginia

Of all the exciting periods of history one of the most overlooked is the Virginia gold rush era . . . the stage was set for it while the earth's first vertebrates began to lumber across the land.

Sometime, during the Ordovician period, a volcano erupted south of what is now Quantico, Virginia. In a series of dramatic convulsions the earth rumbled and shook, cracks began to open and race like snakes across its crust, a mountain peak exhaled black puffs, trembled, and wrenched horribly. Then, with one last explosive shudder, it blew. Earth and rocks and flame red iron spittle soared into the air in a vast black cloud raining down upon the land.

Along with the generation of intense heat, a molten yellow fluid formed, filling the crevices as they opened noisily in the layers of shifting and fracturing rock. It would be eons before men would find this glittering treasure, deposited with such sound and fury, in a place called Virginia.

The recorded history of gold in the state goes back more than two hundred years before America's first gold rush to reports of the precious metal which lured colonists there from England.

Discoveries of enormously rich gold and silver mines in Spain's South American colonies aroused the greed of the English and set them capturing and looting Spanish treasure ships. In 1577, Sir Frances Drake's ship, the *Golden Hind*, successfully attacked the Spanish treasure ship, *Spitfire;*

and it was well worth the chase for the *Spitfire* carried thirteen chests of coins, eighty pounds of pure gold, and twenty-six tons of silver.

Looting the ships of England's rival, Spain, paid well for in 1580, Drake captured another vessel from which he took the equivalent of more than five million dollars in gold and silver.

Sir Walter Raleigh, who also sought gold, writes in his *Discoverie* in 1596 of a fabled King, the furnishings of whose home, table, and kitchen were made entirely of gold and silver. It was tales like this that made the Europeans ready to risk their lives on dangerous ocean voyages across the Atlantic to explore the New World.

Thomas Hariot, one of the first English settlers, reported finding Indians with an abundance of copper, which they used for chains, collars, and drinking cups; and this interested others for they knew copper is sometimes accompanied by gold. Taking for granted that he could profit from vast deposits of gold and silver in Virginia, James I granted the London Company the right "to dig, mine and search for all Manner of Mines of Gold, Silver and Copper" provided they yielded to him "the fifth Part of the same Gold and Silver and the fifteenth Part of all the same Copper."

Gold fever came over with the colonists of Jamestown, Virginia in 1608, and their precarious settlement was tossed like a tiny vessel and almost swamped by the excitement of gold seekers. Labor needed to lay the foundations for a self-sufficient, permanent settlement was ignored. How could anyone work on long-term goals what with excited talk about gold, digging gold, washing gold, refining gold, and loading gold!

Ridicule from Captain John Smith did not stop Captain John Martin and President Christopher Newport from loading a ship with yellow dirt and sending it to London where it was found to be pyrite. Hopes of the English promoters and the colonists died. The real gold was soon discovered to be the gold leaf rather than the gold metal and the next craze in Jamestown involved planting tobacco in every available plot to cure and export to England.

Interest in gold slumbered in Virginia and it was almost two hundred years before it awakened. Nothing is even written of gold until 1826, when Thomas Jefferson reported that a seventeen pennyweight piece was "found on the north side of the Rappahanoc about four miles below the falls" he had no idea that in less than fifty years the confluence of the Rappahannock and the Rapidan rivers would be an important gold mining area.

Among the gentle hills of the Virginia Piedmont in the early 1800s, interest in gold was a drowsing giant beginning to awaken and stretch; and by the 1820s the giant was on a hungry rampage.

Excitement had spread from North Carolina into Virginia and the adjoining states of South Carolina and Georgia; and by 1825 land speculators and prospectors from North Carolina were overflowing into the western half of Virginia. Mining had begun near the falls of the James River and fantastic tales were told of their richness!

According to an article in *Harper's Magazine* there was intriguing evidence that the Virginia placer mines had been worked at a much earlier date and that crucibles for the purpose of melting metal had been used by the Indians or even earlier peoples. The crucibles bore a resemblance to an acorn cup and were obviously for the purpose of melting precious metals.

By 1829 to 1830 thousands of men, women, and children were washing gold throughout western Virginia. Along with the native white Virginians there were Negro slaves, freedmen, Cornish, and German miners working side by side in the pits or along the streams. As has often happened elsewhere, the need for labor and the common need for money made for integration of the races.

Slaves preferred the work in the mines to that in the fields since they were not only sheltered but given additional pay for extra work. There was also a built in opportunity to cache away a nugget now and then and this was done by black and white alike.

Most of the mines were in the gold-pyrite belt of the Southern Appalachians ... that pleasant area of forested hill country that stretches westward from Maryland to east-central Alabama and runs southwesterly from the Potomac. Twelve to twenty-five miles wide and about 140 miles long, the belt extends from Great Falls on the Potomac, southwest through Chancellorsville, Mineral, and Tabscott into Buckingham County. The Virginia gold belt was some four thousand square miles and spread over ten counties.

In the 1830s gold was on everyone's mind even children's. About fifteen miles from Fredericksburg a group of youngsters walking home from Sunday School found a large gold nugget at the edge of the road near the Woodville Mine. News of the children's find in Orange County traveled quickly and people rushed there to begin prospecting. Judge Coalter who owned the mine decided to work it more energetically and with only eight laborers, he had made a profit of ten thousand dollars in ten months.

By the 1830s mining was the leading industry in the South and its mines were estimated to be producing about five million dollars a year.

Many of the mines were worked by farmers during the season when the crops did not demand their labors. Census figures list as "miners" only employees in mines such as the Woodville or the Vaucluse; therefore they show far fewer people listed as miners than there actually were. Many men thought of themselves as farmers rather than gold miners although they worked a digging on their farm.

But there were others who were full-time miners from the very beginning and entire families, Negro slaves and freedmen, Cornish and German miners worked side by side along the streams and in the placer pits.

They used simple tools: picks, axes, shovels, and spades for digging out the gold bearing sand and gravel, and pans, longtoms, or rockers for washing the sand and gravel so that the gold, or color as they sometimes called it, would settle to the bottom. When no water was nearby, they carried the gravel to streams in buckets, baskets, wheelbarrows, and carts. At first there was an abundance of placer gold and in Louisa County one farmer with his three slaves washed out about one thousand dollars per day.

Later, entrepreneurs who had invented more sophisticated gold-washing methods than panning brought in machines using horse, water, or steam power and would contract with a mine owner for a percentage of the profits to allow him to use their invention.

As placer pits were depleted, shafts were sunk and vein mines were opened; rock was dug out and hoisted to the surface in barrels to be crushed by the monstrous iron discs of the noisy stamp machines. Power rollers and steam engines were purchased, skilled engineers employed, and large amounts of capital invested.

Mines incorporated as they became more permanent industries in Virginia. A Spotsylvania County mine where shafts were sunk 150 feet employed fifty laborers, among them skilled Cornish miners. After expenses the net in-

come for the year was twelve thousand dollars. Another
mine, the Belzoro, yielded four hundred dollars a day from
one crushing machine and six stamp mills.

Among the famous mines in Fauquier County were the
Embry, the Emigold near the town of Goldvein, the Franklin
north of the Rappahannock River about three miles from
Morrisville, the Liberty Hill and the Little Elliot all within a
short distance of Morrisville, the United States Mine in
Western Spotsylvania County on the south side of the Rappahannock River about twelve miles from Fredericksburg,
and the Whitehall in Spotsylvania County one and a half
miles northwest of Shady Grove Church.

One of the well known mines in Goochland County was
the Moss about one and a half miles southwest of Tabscott
where early samples indicated the yield of gold to be over
seven dollars per hundred pounds of ore.

In Orange County the famous mines were the Melville,
the Woodville, and the Vaucluse mine eighteen miles west
of Fredericksburg, first worked in 1832. During the depression the Vaucluse was purchased by Henry Ford. The
Vaucluse and the Melville are less than three thousand feet
apart. The Tellurium Mine, one of the first attempts at vein
mining, lies two and a half miles southwest of Tabscott in
continguous parts of Fuvanna and Goochland counties.

By 1834, it was estimated that six million dollars had
already come from the Virginia mines and most of it had
gone abroad to be used in the arts and in jewelry making. A
report in 1836 in the *American Journal of Science* com-
mented that while the state possessed "great mineral trea-
sures . . . they are to be obtained only by sober industry and
skillful application of knowledge and capital." And from
1834 to 1839 thirty-four companies were chartered with
some of the investment coming from local sources but much

from New York and New England, and even a small amount from interests as far away as Great Britain.

Villages sprang up overnight around the mines as log houses were constructed for the laborers and frame for the superintendents and engineers—"respectable gentlemen and master miners" they were sometimes called. Writings of the day comment that "these men compared favorably with those of England in intelligence, zeal and candor."

In the 1830s the miner left his log cabin, shanty, or canvas tent every morning carrying his pick and shovel to work at mines such as the Vaucluse, the Melville, the Tellurium, or the Moss. He carried home about ten dollars pay a month in gold dust which he kept in his clothing or sometimes hidden away in glass bottles. Miners and merchants had small hand scales on which they weighed the gold dust out for purchases, the dust worth about ninety-five cents per pennyweight. In these mining shantytowns the necessities of life might often be absent but there were luxuries such as brandied peaches or oysters to splurge upon.

After the gold was smelted some was sent in bars directly to Europe, some became jewelry, some was taken to the mint at Philadelphia where it was exchanged for coins and some was given by the miners to private minters. Christopher Bechtler of Rutherfordton, North Carolina, who made America's first one dollar gold piece was one of these early trusted miners. When he made his coins he would then stamp them with "Virginia Gold $1.00" or $2.50 or $5.00 and the date.

Reports from the United States Mint show that from 1829 to 1860 over three million dollars worth of Virginia gold was coined at Philadelphia. But since gold went into local trade, was used in the arts and coined by North Carolina's Bechtler Mint, the value amount of Virginia gold is impossible to estimate with exactitude. However, it was well over five million dollars.

Virginia mining stock was in great demand and quoted regularly on the New York Stock Exchange. The stock of one of the Virginia mines was so coveted that it rose from its par value of one hundred dollars per share to one thousand dollars per share and even at this price there were more buyers than shares available! Exaggerated reports spread the excitement about the mines until finally speculators were ruined and the Virginia gold stock bubble burst.

Interest in shaft and hard rock mining began to wane when news of gold in California blazoned in the 1849 newspapers; for miners had visions of quick wealth—gold in streams, nuggets to be picked up in fields, and the abundant placer gold they had found during those first years after gold was discovered in the southeast. The more venturesome miners of Virginia, the Carolinas, and Georgia headed West.

But one hundred and fifty years later there is still gold. For Fredericksburg hardware stores have gold pans for sale, and people may be seen panning and finding "color" in streams such as Wilderness Run and Mine Run near the old, abandoned shafts of Orange County or Little Byrd Creek in Goochland County.

The location of many of the old mines is long since forgotten ... but with new extraction methods some of them may one day come back to life and produce gold in the Virginia Piedmont again.

6.
The Discovery of Gold in South Carolina

Andrew Jackson was president, the final war with England was over, and the wild Indians remaining, such as the Comanche and Apache, were out West. From many aspects Colonel Benjamin Haile found 1827 a good time to be alive as he strolled along beside a stream that bordered his plantation in Lancaster County.* He was watching the water and casually looking for fish when his attention was drawn to a rock embedded in the bank that glittered brightly.

He weighed it, he bit it, he had it assayed, and he discovered that it was a gold nugget.

The Colonel was not unfamiliar with gold for he knew that gold mining had been going on almost thirty years to the north near Charlotte, North Carolina, in fact since 1801 after its discovery in Cabarrus County.

Following his discovery of the nugget that he had spied by chance the Colonel conducted a profitable placer mine for many years at the site of what would someday prove one of the southeast's richest gold mines, producing over six and a half million dollars in gold. Gold was later found in most of the counties in the South Carolina Piedmont with the largest and most productive mines in three main areas: Lancaster and Chesterfield counties; in the Smyrna area of both York and Cherokee where there were at least fifty diggings; and McCormick County and adjacent Abbeville and Greenville.

---

*Present-day South Carolina county names are used for location purposes.

At the Haile the lode or source of the gold, as might be expected, was very close to the heaviest concentration of placers. The Colonel never really found the vein but he did notice that the gold tended to collect in the stream channel where the current was the most turbulent and the lighter pebbles swept away. After the vein was found and much later in 1883 it was estimated that the gold per ton averaged .55 ounce but over the years as the Haile was mined there was undoubtedly a progressive decrease in the amount of gold ore close to the surface. There was also a variation for rich streaks found in different parts of the mine to a depth of at least two hundred feet contained from .6 ounce to 2 ounces per ton.

O. M. Lieber writing of the Haile Mine in 1858 says that nuggets were found there worth from three hundred to five hundred dollars, but no records were kept. The estimated total production was almost three and a half million dollars by the early 1900s.

Almost as famous as the Haile was the Brewer Mine in Chesterfield County just west of Jefferson on a ridge that runs between Lynch's River and Little Fork Creek and covers almost 1,400 acres.

Discovered about the same time as the Haile, the Brewer was mined continuously and by 1843, after the main vein or lode was discovered, as many as two hundred miners in groups of three to six were each mining a plot of land twelve feet square according to the terms of their leases. Although there is no information available on the gold content of the ore during the early days, some of the "pay dirt" must have been extremely rich because the miners in California would have considered this a very small claim.

In McCormick persistence paid off for William Dorn and his brother, Captain James Dorn, who after years of exploratory digging struck gold in 1852 in what is now practically the middle of town. Some three hundred thousand dollars worth of gold was taken out at a cost of only twelve hundred dollars and the Dorn mine became the state's second largest producer after the Haile.

Before the Civil War there were twenty-one working mines in Chesterfield and Lancaster counties, nineteen mines in operation in Spartanburg, Union, and York counties, while Greenville and Pickens counties had eight working placer mines. Abbeville and Edgefield counties had ten working mines which made a total of fifty-eight operating mines before the energies of South Carolinians were turned to the Confederate cause.

The Civil War virtually ruined mining in South Carolina for more than a decade. And during the eleven-year occupation of the state by federal troops there was little interest on the part of the citizens in showing the Yankees where the mines were. The Haile had been converted to copper during the war and many other mines were abandoned for lack of manpower.

Sherman had a particularly bitter hatred for South Carolina and on his march of devastation through the state, one of his acts was to send a detachment of troops to destroy and burn the buildings and equipment at the Haile.

There are periodic resurgences of gold mining in South Carolina such as at Winnsboro and Jefferson and the current mining of both gold and silver at the Haile continues with a modest measure of success. Today, the Haile land resembles a desolate moonscape save for the area occupied by the present-day mining corporation. During its long history it has been worked by both open-cut and underground methods which have left the area scarred by open pits such as the Bumalo and Blue Pool. Some of the vertical shafts are as deep as five hundred feet. Embracing four square miles and located in Lancaster County, three and one half miles northeast of Kershaw and fifty-five miles north of Columbia, it was the most successful gold-mining operation and largest single producer of gold in the Appalachian region.

In addition to the Haile, Brewer, and Dorn mines there were many other prospects. Some of the better known were the DeSoto prospect in Greenville County, which local legend links with the Spanish explorer de Soto; the Cureton Mine near Greer; the Westmoreland Mine and Wild Cat mines north of Greenville; the Young Mine at Troy; the Lamar Mine north of Camden; the Belk Mine north of Lancaster; the Blackmon Mine east of Kershaw; the Funderburk Mine north of Jefferson; the Rabon Creek prospect west of Laurens; the Henckel and Jesse Lay mines near Walhalla; the Culbreath Mine south of Newberry; the Barnett, Wilson, and Campbell mines north of York; and a multitude of others particularly in the Smyrna area and Hickory Grove.

The states that led in gold production in the southeast were North Carolina which was known as "The Golden State" for fifty years before California, Georgia, and South Carolina in that order. If the figures of total production from the southeastern mines seem small, there are a number of reasons.

One was the fact that in the early 1830s, the first years some of these prospects and mines were operated, no production records were kept. For example none from this period are available from the Brewer Mine which was reportedly discovered in 1828 and known in 1830 as one of the most productive mines in the area employing as many as two hundred miners.

Another reason was lack of technology in the South and the fact that many of the prospects and mines were being operated by farmers! Western mines came along a quarter of a century or more later and therefore mining technology was considerably more advanced. After the placer days were over the Western mines were soon being run by experts versed in deep shaft mining and hydraulic mining. Mine owners out West were not economically devastated by the Civil War and a subsequent lack of financial resources to reopen their mines as were many owners in the South.

Western mines were also much better capitalized throughout the entire first half of the twentieth century and able to purchase more sophisticated equipment. For example, North Carolina's Gold Hill, a rich gold bearing area, suffered from a lack of capital, little technological know-how, and reckless management.

Lastly, many of the western mines continued on into the mid-1950s while most of the southeastern mines folded at the time of World War II and later, unable to pay the higher wages workers expected after working in defense industries, could not reopen.

7.
They Called Me "Fool Billy"

They called me "Fool Billy" and said that I would never find gold. Born the grandson of German immigrants in upcountry South Carolina, I built my plantation on Hard Labor Creek. Some folks thought I had lived up to the name of that creek and others thought I just got lucky.

There was talk about gold up in North Carolina from as far back as I can remember and in 1828, like everyone else, I was excited about Ben Haile's panning gold out of the stream on his land near Kershaw. That was the same year they found gold on the Brewer property in Chesterfield District . . . droves of miners began going up and down the streams of upcountry South Carolina.

Over at Smyrna in York District men were out in the woods prospecting so thick they bumped elbows panning along the stream banks. I traveled up there and watched them myself. Then, four years later, a fellow named Zeig showed me one of the prettiest specimens of gold you ever saw and said he had panned it out of a branch running through John Hearst's land right near my place.

From the time I laid eyes on that little nugget I couldn't think about anything else; and the next few years, I didn't pay any mind to planting crops . . . I hunted for gold and spent my time panning Persimmon Branch.

Every day I'd get out there in that creek and slowly and carefully work my way upstream. Most of the time I'd find some and then a day came when I couldn't see any more color in my pan. Next day was the same. I've passed it, I said,

68

angry with myself, and went back until it wasn't long before I thought I knew where it was coming from.

Sure enough, I had pinpointed the location of rich ore deposits and when I did, I went to old man John Wardlaw Hearst. I told Mr. John I had found a rich vein and I said, "I'll show you right where that gold is, if you'll let me have an interest in it. How about it?"

But all he did was shake his head and say, "Fool Billy, what crazy notion are you going to come up with next?" He leaned back in his rocker on that big piazza of his and he cackled fit to kill.

But the more he thought about the chance he had to sell me that land at a good price, the more he couldn't resist. Course, I didn't have any money and all I could do was offer to buy it on time. But what did he have to lose? If I couldn't pay for it, he'd get his land back.

I signed a note to purchase over 1,300 acres. Some folks sniggered behind my back and others felt sorry for me and purty soon I was beginning to do some worrying myself. It was getting hard just to feed the slaves I had out there panning every day; and I tried to take decent care of them.

One Sunday morning in the early spring of 1852 I was sitting in church and that day I was beginning to believe the nickname of "Fool Billy" was right. Next day my plantation and all my slaves were to be placed on the auction block in Edgefield for back taxes. Today was Sunday and by tomorrow night, I wouldn't hardly have a plug a tobacco left . . . no land, no slaves . . . much less any gold.

After preachin', I went up to the house and was sitting eating field peas and cornbread while the men were out digging just like they had every day for months. I was feeling mighty low about the sale coming up next day and then it happened. I heard somebody hollerin' loud as they could, "Master Bill, Master Bill!"

The first thing I thought was that one of the men had been hurt bad so I jumped up from the table and hurried out on the back porch. There was Elias, a big strapping slave and one of my best miners. He held out his gold pan to me and his grin was a crescent moon in a dark sky. The bottom of the pan was covered with fine grained gold!

I knew we'd found the rich vein we'd been looking for and my next thought was how to stop that sale? We didn't have much time for it was about a two day ride. I rode to the mine and found the best man I had and put him on my fastest horse. "Hurry!" I said. "And when you get to that Courthouse, tell them to stop the sale right away. We've struck gold." He galloped away and reached the Courthouse just in time to keep them from auctioning off my property.

From then on the mine produced up to nine thousand dollars a day. 'Course, some of the gold went to the Dahlonega mint and some lined the miner's pockets but it wouldn't have been right to make those hardworking men put it all in the mint. Why they were the ones that had found the nuggets and the good ore. Who could blame a slave or an Irishman if he saw something he wanted to buy and he traded a little ore for it. Others took off to rest for awhile or to see the sights up North and came back with handfuls of cash they had traded for gold. But I say, why shouldn't they get rich, too? There was enough gold for all of us.

Overnight I became a millionaire and one of the first things I had always wanted was to live in one of them big houses with white columns. I had a fellow draw me a picture of a fine home ... so fine it took my slaves seven years to build; and when it was completed, I named it

"Oakgrove." Most of the house is morticed and the only nails I would let them use were wrought iron.

I wanted to put gold shingles on the roof but you know how the government's always snooping in a man's business and stopping you from doing something if they can. Here I was in Dornville, a town named after myself; and I couldn't even put the kind of shingles I wanted on my own house!

Now, all those years I tried not to think about women folk. Girls never had much time for me, nor I for them but when I saw beautiful, fifteen-year-old Martha Jane Rutledge from Greenville, I knew I wanted to marry her and for some reason she said "yes." I made up my mind there would never be another wedding like it. If you read the *Greenville Southern Patriot* afterward, maybe you'd agree. The paper said the wedding supper was big enough for a thousand people and the writer called "Mattie"—my nickname for Martha—an "Eastern princess." Just imagine that! "Fool Billy" marrying a girl that looked like an "Eastern Princess."

I haven't lived here all my life without knowing how people in a small town think . . . every one of 'em wondering what rich old Billy was going to pay the preacher . . . and I made a vow myself, I'd give then a real show. When the service was over I went up to the preacher with his payment. I stretched out my hand and handed him a pair of new kid gloves. You should have heard the disappointed gasp from folks standing nearby and I seen everyone just a gawking at us.

That preacher had the funniest look on his face and I put my fingers up, like I was stroking my mustache, to keep him from seeing my smile. He tried to thrust the fingers of his right hand into one of the gloves. He pushed and he strug-

Billy Dorn panned for years, never becoming discouraged.
Harper's New Monthly Magazine, 1857

gled and he pushed some more, but for the life of him he couldn't get his fingers in that glove. I began to shake all over from trying not to laugh. Finally, he poked a finger in to see what was stuffed down there and what do you know . . . he pulled out a gold nugget!

You should have heard folks' oh's and the ah's. The Reverend brought out one gold nugget after another from the fingers of the gloves while everybody crowded around him. I had tried to see that each finger had around five hundred dollars worth of gold in it.

Gold has always brought me a lot of fun. One time I was on my way back to Oakgrove from the Philadelpia Mint and stopped over in Greenville to see my cousin. He's a long faced, serious-minded Baptist if ever I knew one. I lugged two big suitcases into the house and they were filled to overflowing with gold pieces. To see what he would say, I opened them up, reached in and tossed him a few coins. At first he looked like he was going to keel over from pure shock. Then his face just lit up like a lantern; and he smiled, more tickled than I've ever seen him before or since.

I enjoy being rich but money isn't everything. Sometimes all the things you own can be mighty hard to keep up with. My slaves, for instance. I would see one I couldn't place for the life of me and walk up to him and say, "Who you belong to?" He'd look at me surprised and say, "Why, I belong to you, Master Billy." But when you have almost two hundred slaves how in tarnation can you remember all of 'em?

When the "War of Northern Aggression" came, like any good South Carolinian, I wanted to fight, but at my age I wasn't able to do that. So, I did the next best thing. I outfitted a company of our boys to go after those Yankees and teach them a thing or two. It didn't work out that way though and it makes my heart heavy to think about it even now. Here in South Carolina, the War just went from bad to worse. Before long, the Yankee soldiers took everything including my gold mine. There was plenty of good ore left but they shipped it off to pave roads all over the country . . . imagine, paving roads with my gold!

By the time Lee surrendered I didn't have the energy to mine the way I use to in the old days. Everything had changed. There were no more slaves and no more Irishmen to work the diggings so I leased the mine to General Joe Wheeler. I admired Wheeler for being a fine general, but I had to admit, he wasn't much of a gold miner. After he left, the only men that came to talk to me about leasing it were nothing but triflin' carpetbaggers! There wasn't one of 'em a June bug couldn't beat diggin' for gold. Why, I got over two million dollars from that mine myself and I know there was still gold there.

Finally, all I could do was sell out. That fellow, Cyrus McCormick, who invented the reaper bought it in 1874. Maybe he will do better, but I doubt that.

You know, sometimes I sit on the piazza here at "Oakgrove" and look out over those woods and chuckle to myself . . . about how they used to poke fun at me during the early years . . . and all the time, under that tangle of brush covered with honeysuckle the gold was just sitting there waiting for "Fool Billy."

In 1876, two years after selling the mine to McCormick, Dorn died. Although he was short and considered somewhat plain in appearance, he was a good humored, gentlemanly fellow and well liked. At the height of his career he owned a plantation, a gold mine, a hotel and was a member of the South Carolina legislature. A century afterward Billy Dorn is still an unforgettable South Carolinian, remembered not only for his wealth and generosity but for his colorful character.

One of the region's most intriguing unanswered questions is what happened to Billy Dorn's gold mine? Why did it produce so abundantly for him, but refuse to yield its precious metal to later owners? Is there a chance that the miles of virtually unknown, unmapped tunnels underneath McCormick (as Dornsville was later named) might someday bestow their hidden treasure on yet another Billy Dorn?

The government estimate of the gold under the little town is a million and a quarter dollars, a foundation of, perhaps, untold millions secreted in the earth on which McCormick is built. "Oakgrove," Dorn's impressive, white columned home, burned in 1935, but people still dig among the ruins for chests of gold they believe are buried there.

8.
Scarlett O'Hara of the Dorn Mine

The big, brawny young fellow leaned against the doorway of the pocket-size log cabin and looked adoringly at the girl beside him. Glossy black curls fell riotously about her shoulders, her skin was a luminous, creamy white and her brown eyes had sparks in them.

"When will I see you again? Tomorrow night?" he pleaded.

"I may be busy tomorrow night sewing or churning butter, Hans."

"Marietta, don't put me off. You know I want to marry you."

He gently turned her toward him and the cold February night caused the delicate white mist of her breath to float seductively in the air between them.

"We could have our own little house on my land. Abbeville District has good farm land. We would work hard together and have many fine children," and here he stammered slightly with embarrassment.

"Work together on your farm? Why these hands were never meant for rough work, Hans." Marietta was staring at her hands thoughtfully.

"You know, Hans, your land is near Dorn's Gold Mine. Maybe you have gold too."

"Mr. Dorn is wasting his time. He hasn't found any gold yet. Don't you care for me a little?"

"Care for you? Why, of course I do," she replied, leaning toward him ever so slightly her red lips curving enticingly. Then she glided through the door and into the cabin, turned and cracking it almost imperceptibly whispered, "Good-night, dear Hans."

That night Marietta tossed restlessly thinking of the men who worked in the gold mines. Like Hans, her parents were farmers and what did they have to show for all their labor? Her mother's face was lined and worn, her father's hands calloused from the plow. Was this the life for her?

Miner's daughters wore fine dresses and bright ribbons on their bonnets. They went to places like London and Paris and came back with exciting stories. The only way to live like that would be to marry the son of one of the wealthy miners. If she did not think of some bold plan, she would become as dull and mealy-mouthed as her sister Ilse.

It was not long afterward that her father came back from the store with exciting news. Dorn had struck it rich and everyone was talking about it. Soon a Chilean mill operated by two mules was working fifteen bushels of ore a day from the mines.

Often Marietta went up to the loft early with Ilse but only because the darkness gave her the opportunity to think uninterrupted. She looked toward the other bed con-temptuously. Her sister must be asleep. The corn shuck mattress like her own was just a few feet away but the two girls might have had an ocean between them and been born to different parents.

Ilse's face had none of the rippling expressions that came with lightning swift changes of mood nor did she have the beautiful coloring and coquettish ways of her younger sis-ter. Her long flaxen hair and almost too fair complexion ran true to her long line of Saxon ancestors.

Serious and hardworking by nature, Ilse had been given more responsibility by her mother. To Anna Kirsch, Mar-ietta was like some beautiful, frivolous doll which she could admire but never quite call her own. There had been many times she had not known how to handle this daughter.

One night in late June, Ilse lay in her bed scarcely daring to breathe. She heard Marietta tossing but did not want her to know she was awake lest it arouse the other girl's curiosity. Ilse's heart held a secret that would have surprised Marietta. In fact, if she suspected it she would probably make her younger sister's life even more miserable.

The next day after the mid-day meal was cleared away and the girls had tidied the kitchen together, Marietta went up the ladder to the loft to turn the mattresses. She had begun to lay her plans.

This is where she was when the sound of boots struck the wooden plank steps of the cabin. Ilse went to the door and upstairs Marietta could hear Hans' hopeful voice asking for her. She made a small tight fist with her right hand and then she composed herself and went down the ladder.

Hans was talking with Ilse but when he saw Marietta, joy flooded his face. Ilse went over to the hearth and busied herself with the pots and trivets.

Marietta was full of hints about wanting to go berry-picking as if she were afraid to go alone. Hans picked up this cue eagerly. Ilse was amazed for if ever anyone was reluctant to stain their fingers with berry juice, it was Marietta. How strangely she had behaved in the last day or two. Her tawny eyes sparkled and she seemed almost feverish.

The next afternoon Marietta put on her prettiest bonnet. Ilse watched her tie the ribbon carefully arranging the bow at one side of her lovely face. Then she removed the bark bucket from the hook and without so much as a good-bye to Ilse or her mother, Marietta set out. She was to meet Hans at the log bridge near the edge of the woods. Persimmon

Branch was the boundary line between the Kirsch property and that of their neighbors.

Just beyond the log bridge a narrow path wound through woods pitted with placer pits. Amid the underbrush of scrub oaks, cedars, and sweetgum scores of miners dug for ore. Others burrowed slope tunnels in the side of the hill or sunk vertical shafts. These shafts gaped dark and treacherous and unwary animals sometimes plunged down into them. Unable to climb up the hard, steep clay walls they starved to death.

In her bright yellow dress, Marietta was a splash of sunlight among the trees.

"I'll pick berries over there," she called to Hans as she pointed to a grove of oaks," and you pick down along the branch. Let's see who can pick the most!"

As she gathered berries, Marietta gradually edged deeper into the woods.

"Marietta" Hans was calling her.

"I'll be there in a minute," she answered as she moved farther away. She knew he could no longer see her. She must hurry! Less than a mile away, in the direction of Edgefield, was the house of a very wealthy miner and his sons.

"Mar-ee-et-a, Mar-ee-et-a!" It was that irritating Hans again. But she turned in a direction he wouldn't expect. He could never find her now! Peevishly, she wondered how long he would go on calling.

Her father had mentioned the family one day, pointing out the rock chimney that could be seen in the winter from the road. Surely there must be a trail cutting across the woods for she was now parallel to the wagon road. Hans' voice could still be heard in the distance. She did not turn back.

Marietta's feet found the ruts of a road. She was excited for surely the house could not be far away now. It must be an old wagon road seldom used now for it was much over-grown. Perhaps she had lost her way. She went on until she reached the edge of a clearing and there was the house before her. Now that the time had come to carry out her plan, Marietta trembled a little.

She stepped back deeper into the underbrush of sweet-gum trees and scrub oaks and gave her hair a quick flutter-ing pat. A transformation came over her. The self-possessed coquette was now a helpless, frightened girl. Marietta stepped out into the clearing and as she did one of the miner's sons rounded the corner of the house leading his horse.

"Oh, sir. Please help me." She took a few steps toward him, and swayed as if about to faint. Immediately the tall young man reached out to steady this lovely, frightened creature.

"Who are you, sir?" she said looking up at him her face not far from his.

"You'd better sit down for a minute, miss. I'm Eric Shinn. Who are you?"

"My name is Marietta, Marietta Kirsch. I'm afraid I have gotten myself terribly turned around."

"And somewhat scratched by briars," said the young man looking down at Marietta's ankles. For the first time she noticed that there were tiny flecks of blood where her flesh was pierced by thorns but it made her story seem all the more true.

"Are you the daughter of Wilhelm Kirsch?" Marietta nodded.

"I know your father. We have met over at the store near Dorn's Gold Mines. I would ask you to come in and rest but mother was taken a year ago and we men have little comfort to offer a young lady. Here, have a dipper of water."

As he lifted it to her lips she raised a hand to steady the gourd and her eyes looked deep into his.

"I'll saddle the stallion and take you home."

"Oh, do you know where my house is?"

"It's on the other side of Persimmon Branch just beyond the log bridge, isn't it? I believe I've seen you near that bridge." With Hans, she thought and for a moment there was a stab of fear. Would he think she was already spoken for?

As soon as the horse was saddled they were on their way. Marietta noticed Eric's leisurely pace and desire to talk. He was prolonging the trip and she had the opportunity to be her most winsome and beguiling self. The closer they came to the Kirsch cabin the more slowly the horse's feet seemed to move and a ten minute ride became much longer. As they rode up to the clearing where the house stood, Eric asked if he might come to call.

Marietta hesitated with feigned shyness and then, eyes downward, she nodded. Within a short time Eric became a frequent visitor at the Kirsch home. Hans was more and more distraught for he either found Eric there when he arrived or Marietta was so involved with some task for her mother that she had no time for him.

Finally, Hans pleaded with Ilse to intercede for him.

"I will be at the bridge at Persimmon Branch at sunset. Please, promise you will get Marietta to meet me." Ilse promised. She found Marietta irritated and reluctant but she admonished her.

"If you aren't going to marry Hans you should tell him so."

"The silly fellow. I've never told him I would."

"He's breaking his heart over you. Tell him you aren't going to marry him!" Tell him so that he will get over a girl like you. Tell him so that he can love me she thought and she blushed at her own reasons for wanting to help Hans. Finally, her sister agreed to go.

After the supper pots and pans were washed, Marietta went out with the pretext of looking for her favorite kitten and Ilse followed at a safe distance. Hans was already there. She watched them and could even hear some of his words as he pleaded with Marietta. She was filled with conflict and suspense. Why was her sister so irresistible?

Should she have given him this opportunity to speak with Marietta? She began to suffer dreadfully. Surely, her sister would realize what a fine young man he was and give in to his pleas. How jealous she was! Why was Marietta taking so long? It was dark by now and still they continued to talk. The moon came out and Ilse could see two dark figures silhouetted near the bridge.

Suddenly hoof beats were heard and Ilse saw Marietta dart into the woods. She must think it was Eric. He would not take kindly to her meeting another man. Hans did not move. She stood staring in the direction of the hoof beats.

Eric rode toward the bridge. Evidently a tree must have concealed Hans for the young miner on horseback appeared not to see him. Eric turned his horse into the woods toward the stone smelting furnace. There he stopped and as the horse stamped and snorted restlessly, Eric began to call softly.

"Marietta, Marietta."

They must be meeting here but how could Marietta join her sweetheart with Hans only a few feet away? This should certainly be enough to show Hans she had no love for him, thought Ilse. She settled herself more comfortably to see what would happen. Ilse was sure Hans would step into view any moment but he must be remaining as still as she.

Eric walked his horse this way and that and then tethered him and sat down upon the low wall of the smelting furnace. She was getting cold but she was more afraid Hans would hear her now than Eric. He was too far away. Finally, he mounted his horse and in a moment was gone.

Ilse saw Hans go past and she followed as quickly as she dared. What a relief it was to get home. Of course, Marietta was not there but she was sure she would be soon. She awoke late that night and listened for her sister's breathing from the mattress a few feet away but heard nothing. For the first time she felt a stab of panic. Had Eric found her and taken her away with him?

It was the next morning before Anna and Wilhelm Kirsch discovered their daughter's absence. Ilse seemed as amazed as they. Marietta did not come home all day nor that night. The second morning a search party combed the banks of Persimmon Branch and even the Dorn Mines area but could find no trace of her.

During the weeks that followed Hans often dropped by the Kirsch home and Ilse was always consoling and attentive. The following spring they became engaged. One summer evening while they were walking along a path at the edge of Persimmon Branch Hans stopped abruptly.

"Did you hear that? he said and plunged into the woods. Ilse waited in amazement. Soon he was back.

"It was a girl crying out. I heard it. I know I did."

"There was nothing, Hans."

"Yes. I saw it. There was a flash of light among the trees, a glowing, yellowish light."

"It was a miner walking along with his lantern."

"No, somehow it reminded me of Marietta."

Ilse's heart began to beat uncomfortably fast.

"How silly. No one has seen or heard from Marietta. She must have found herself a gold miner!" And then she wished she could recall her stinging words for Hans did not reply nor did he place his arm around her waist on the way home.

A few months after they were married Hans was walking through the woods one gray winter afternoon when he saw a glowing bit of color a short distance away through the trees. A piece of sunlight appeared to be lying on the ground but, of course, it was not really sunlight. Instead, the rays were striking a piece of yellow fabric.

Hans reached down to pick it up, and as he did his left boot gave way beneath him. He pulled back instantly realizing he must be on the rim of an abandoned mine shaft. Some were up to seventy-five-feet deep. He had almost pitched into it head first. What a horrible death that would be he thought. Cautiously, he poked a long stick toward the bit of yellow caught on a branch that lay across the top of the shaft.

After a few trys he was successful. He shook the leaves from it and looked at it with a sense of horror, recognizing it immediately. It was the yellow shawl Marietta had worn the night she disappeared for he had seen it many times. With horror, he knew what had happened. It was too tragic to tell Ilse for he knew how dearly she had loved her sister.

For the first time, he understood the strange story the miners had begun to tell. How, after leaving their diggings at dusk, they would meet a beautiful girl in a golden yellow dress. For a while she would walk along nearby enticing them with her loveliness. Then, just as they were about to come close and embrace her, she would turn and run coquettishly.

While she could still be seen among the tree trunks, her feet appeared to leave the earth and finally she turned into a misty, golden revenant floating through the woods in the distance. Some had sworn they would catch her if it was the last thing they ever did.

They ran through the woods hungrily in pursuit, tripping, falling, getting up to run again, thorns tearing their clothes and scratching their faces. How few girls there were who looked like this one in the South Carolina gold fields!

Over the years there were many who reported seeing her. And even when he was an old man Hans would sometimes take the path uphill through the woods, blanketed with the leaves of great oaks, poplars, and hickorys, their trunks shining silver in the moonlight.

He would stare hopefully all around him and call, "Marietta, Marietta. I know you're there. Please. Just let me see you one more time." And tears would flow down his wrinkled cheeks. But she never appeared again to her faithful Hans.

Now wasn't that just like Marietta?

In Abbeville County today, above one of the old Dorn Gold Mines, is a long, low ridge covered with large oaks and sweet gums. In the span of history it really wasn't so long ago that Marietta met Hans and Eric here.

At dusk when the wind blows and leaves crackle and scrape against each other does a lovely girl in a golden dress sometimes toss her head and flirt and float along the ridge beneath the whispering boughs? Who can say? Only the trees stand tall, mysterious, and all-knowing.

9.
The Future of Cap'n Thies

From the vantage point of the Victorian bed where Dr. Adolph Thies was propped up with pillows, he observed with pleasure the beautiful old mahogany chest and above it his favorite Vermeer painting. On the walls were diplomas from famous schools of mining in Germany, and mementos from mines in North Carolina, Georgia, and Alabama where he had worked in managerial or consulting positions.

A chaise and chairs were strewn with a profusion of pillows: footstools were everywhere and on the table was a Meissen tea set. Here were all the exquisite objects he had collected, the comforting clutter with which a German of his means and taste liked to surround himself. And then the objects began to fade. . . .

In these last few minutes before Dr. Thies' death he was imagining himself back in the house at Kershaw, back in the old days of the Haile Mine. The room is somewhat darker than usual he thought to himself but he felt very satisfied for the house seemed to him to be the finest in the little South Carolina town and he was proud of the way it sat upon the hill overlooking the mine and the village. The faces around him were those of the people he loved. There was his daughter seated in a chair near him and his boys Gus, Oscar, and Adolph . . . but where was Ernest?

Where was the son he had trained to follow in his own footsteps? Everyone was there except for him. No matter. Ernest was always preoccupied with work and the mine and as he had often told him. "Dat is goot. You vill go far,

Ernest." Ernest had the best education money could buy, all the spending money he wanted and the whole family knew he loved him above any of his other sons. Adolph Thies felt as if he might be going to sleep before the boy got here for he was drifting off now. But he was sure he would see him soon . . . soon . . . soo . . . and, so he would. He was dying and in these last moments his thoughts had slipped back, back to more than a decade ago . . . the years before Ernest was gone.

A moment later a nurse bustled in and a frenzy of activity began in the big Myers Park house at Charlotte, North Carolina. It was 1917 and the great Dr. Adolph Thies, world famous metallurgist, was dead. Educated in mining in Germany at Liegen, Giesen, and Carlsruhe he was drawn like a magnet to America during the gold rush years; and his fame had spread across the southern states from the Carolinas to Alabama.

Dr. Adolph's last great challenge came in his old age. It was 1887 when he arrived at the Haile Mine, South Carolina's richest gold field and, perhaps, one of the richest in the southeast. Although an aging man, he had never lost his dreams and now he was consumed with a new ambition, how to better extract gold from the low-grade sulfide ores left after the early, more accessible gold. His son, Ernest, was equally absorbed, joining in all the experiments for a process that would rescue the famous mine, and turn it into a profitable operation.

Within a few years the mill capacity was increased as surveys discovered richer veins and larger ore bodies. Dr. Thies' optimistic goal of "100 tons a day" became a reality by the early 1890s. He not only made the Haile—Adolph Thies was the Haile. By the turn of the century his mine was famous and there were visits from the best-known mining engineers of the day.

"Ernest, I've trained you and it is time for you to take over management of the mine," he had said one afternoon. His energies were flagging and in 1904 Dr. Thies would retire to Charlotte. Ernest was stamped with the same sense of purpose but he knew he must prove himself.

"They don't trust me yet in New York," he thought. "They don't know whether I can handle responsibility like my father did."

So much of his time was spent planning how to improve the yield. At night he read and kept up on mining developments throughout the world and during the day he continued to pursue both open cut and pit mining with a vengeance. But his real hope for the greater financial backing the mine needed lay in discovering the right place to sink the diamond drill in the ground and bring up treasure. He was eager to discover ever richer ore and each new core sample was carefully analyzed.

No one drove himself any harder than did Ernest and what he required of himself, he required of all others. When he took over management of the Haile the men respected him and it was not long before they called him "Cap'n" Thies.

On the hottest of days he was immaculate in his white linen suit, wearing a wing collar with a looped ascot tie under his resolute chin and carrying a black silk umbrella. When Captain Thies paused to talk to someone on his inspection rounds, the contrast was startling between the rough miners and the slim, impeccable figure in white.

Even his big yellow house on top of the hill was characterized by awe inspiring splendor; for within servants in white mess jackets scurried about ministering to his every need and, of course, those of his guests. Important visitors from the north and officials from New York came and went;

but Ernest Thies never fraternized with his employees and few from the Haile Mine or the town of Kershaw more than glimpsed the interior of "the big house."

News of elegant entertaining would sometimes leak out through the Captain's black chef and maitre d', "Bell" Horton. A newspaper editor who was his dinner guest once wrote that he had never met a more congenial and polished gentleman and that he exuded true hospitality. Although whiskey drinking was quite common in the rough mining village, the Captain enjoyed his lager and even a tot of "schnapps" at home but he never drank a drop in public.

A bachelor but no playboy, Ernest Thies was a man of principle. Some say he was once engaged to a vibrant, brown-haired woman who had come down with her brother to visit from New York, but no wedding plans were ever announced. Perhaps, it was because she had realized that Thies' true love was the Haile.

There were always rumors about the gold production of the mine. Some said that it produced one thousand dollars a day. One day at the mine the Captain was cornered by a visiting sightseer who asked probing questions about how much money the Haile was making. Thies grew angry, cursed him soundly and had him bodily removed from the premises. Everyone believed that the Haile was owned by a New York syndicate but little information reached the public. The truth of what was going on at the mine would always be the Captain's secret.

Kershaw was a typical gold mining community with its excesses and wild, loose ways. None of this sinfulness escaped one of the characters of the mine, Frank Pearson, a helper in the concentrator room who was also something of a fortune teller. Pearson was liked but he was also derided and to some degree even feared. His weather forecasts and fortunes were uncannily accurate but his most frequent and dire prediction was that wickedness would not go unpunished.

"A day of judgement is coming when this Sodom and Gomorrah will sink into a mine shaft and this den of evil will be no more." Pearson would say. His brown eyes would glare, panning from one face to another around him, and he would repeat it again if his audience did not seem sufficiently impressed. Of course, this pronouncement was greeted with loud guffaws and derision.

Monday morning, August 10, 1908, dawned clear and hot like so many summer days in the South Carolina upcountry. When Ernest waked he realized with surprise that it was almost eight o'clock. It was unusual for him not to rise earlier but he had slept poorly the night before and this morning he got up filled with a vague sense of depression. Of all things, he had dreamed of that crazy Frank Pearson, whom he had met on his rounds the Friday before. There were times he was tempted to fire Pearson for he despised his palm readings and infernal prophecies.

Usually, he arose eagerly looking forward to his inspection tour at the mine but not this morning. Whether it was the prolonged and oppressive heat wave that was stifling the South Carolina upcountry or his unpleasant dream of the night before, he lacked his usual enthusiasm.

Ernest bathed, looked through the rack inside the mahogany wardrobe, carefully selecting a fresh white linen suit and dressed with his usual care. Before leaving the dim light of the front hall which received only the rays of the afternoon sun, he stopped at the umbrella rack and from his collection chose a black silk umbrella with an initialed gold handle. His fair Teutonic skin burned easily and the umbrella was a necessity rather than an affectation.

By 8:45 he was headed for his morning inspection tour walking down the road that led through the pines opposite the smelter, the black mushroom bobbing along over his head. As he walked toward the Haile, he continued to diagram a plan he had in mind for more effectively separating the gold from the ore. Was this the reason he was not hurrying more? He had already started out later than usual. But today he almost dreaded having his thoughts interrupted by the routine conversations he would have with the supervisors at each stop after he reached the mine.

Usually he was there at 8:30 but today it would be later, and why should that matter?

At 9:00 he probably should have passed on by and stopped another time to speak to Mrs. L. W. Pittman who was out on her porch sweeping. Instead, he followed an impulse to walk over and compliment her on the thick cream she sent to his cook and stood there chatting for a moment or so. The Pittman's cow was the source of the Captain's daily supply of milk. These pleasantries were a sort of thank you and meant only a small delay, but it was one that would place him that much later at each stop on his rounds through the mine.

At 9:07 Ernest Thies opened the first door of the stamp mill feeling the door vibrate from the thundering rhythm of the iron stamps hammering upon ore. A few minutes later as Mrs. Pittman rested her broom of long rust colored straw against the wall of her porch, she watched him emerge from the second door and approach the engine room which contained the mammoth Corliss 300 horsepower engine. He stuck his head in and saw Pittman, looked up at the big clock on the wall and pulled out his watch saying, "Joe, you're running a little slow, better run her up a couple of minutes."

He paused waiting while Joe Pittman got his stepladder and moved the minute hand of the clock up to 9:10. When Pittman looked around Ernest Thies had turned to leave and was making his way toward the boiler room at the back. He spent only a minute or so with the fireman, Elmo Ogburn, before he left the boiler room and went on to the concentrator room to talk with the supervisor, Mid Truesdale.

It was now about 9:15 A.M. and Truesdale and Captain Thies were conversing a foot or so inside the back door of the concentrator room. In two more minutes the mine would never be the same again.

The stamp mill was a monstrous, noisy dragon its mouth spewing out a tall column of black smoke . . . Joe Pittman, on duty at the throttle of the 300 horsepower Corliss engine, was getting his oil can to oil the big fourteen-foot engine flywheel . . . John and Will Holden were standing watching the ore go through the stamp mill while Elmo Ogburn fired the huge boiler.

"Thanny" Bowers was down in one of the tunnels shoring it up with some timbers and talking to Bob Berrier, about baseball. . . . Wylie Catoe, the "dinkey" engineer was almost ready to leave the mine, his hopper cars loaded with ore . . . the little engine was already impatiently belching forth smoke ready to pull the cars to the stamp mill and Captain Thies was just turning to leave the concentrator room when tragedy struck.

It was swift and unexpected and it had the impact of a bomb and an earthquake combined. Mrs. Pittman heard a sustained angry roar accompanied by a rumble that must have lasted for about five seconds while a wrenching shock went through her house. Looking over at the mine she watched in horror as the fifty-foot tall smokestack separated from the building and collapsed in a massive pile of brick. A big boiler in one of the stamp mills exploded with such force that it turned inside out.

At the same time columns of smoke, clouds of live steam and pieces of metal went in all directions. A stamp mill worker was jerked out the door by the suction, sailed into the air and landed out in the road. Of the building he had left with such appalling suddenness, nothing remained but a pile of rubble.

Then, all was still . . . no more explosions, no outcry, no sound of human voices, just awesome silence. When the smoke lifted the scene was one of shocking destruction. The boiler room, the engine room and the concentrator room had taken the full force of the explosion. They lay, a mass of timbers, brick, and debris, collapsed upon the ground as if smashed flat by a giant fist.

Then there came sounds of life. All at once, workmen began to scramble, stumble and crawl out of the stamp mill coughing and groaning. Like a picture of the last judgement men were appearing almost instantaneously as if they had sprung from the ground. A wave of wives and children surged toward the mine turning up rubble and crying, praying and calling out the names of loved ones. In the mind of the crowd, the flattened remains of engine room spelled death.

When it seemed as if there could be no more left alive a bent figure completely covered with soot and grime crawled from beneath what was left of the stamp mill. His face, arms and body were black and blood streamed from a gash on his head. When he reached Nora Pittman he stopped in front of her.

"Nora, don't you know me? Here I am!" It was Joe Pittman, the boiler room engineer. Weeping with relief, his wife tore off a piece of her petticoat and began cleaning his face and eyes.

"Where is the Cap'n, Nora?"

"He was in the stamp mill but I think he went somewhere else," someone spoke up.

"No. That's not right. He left me and went to the boiler room," said Joe. "We've got to find him."

Then voices in the crowd started saying they had seen him in his white suit in this place or in that helping people. "He was right in the thick of it," called out someone. "Yeah, he was lifting the timbers off one of the men. I seen him for awhile," said Ed Beckham, a laborer. "Then he must 'uv left."

"No, he's still somewhere in the plant and we've got to find him," insisted Pittman.

Those who were not injured began to shovel away the pile of fallen bricks and timbers in the boiler room and found Elmo Ogburn buried in the still warm debris. The fireman was unconscious and had a serious head wound. And then they found Mid Truesdale ... barely alive ... buried under rubble near the door of the concentrator room. Many searchers were still saying the Captain was not in the mill but Pittman believed he was.

There was nothing to do but keep on digging.

About 9:45 someone saw a glint of gold shining amid the bricks. It was not far from where they had found Mid Truesdale and it was the handle of an umbrella. Now they began to burrow furiously by hand certain they were near the body of the Captain. Timbers were hoisted by the rescuers and hot brick and debris removed until, finally, they uncovered Ernest Thies. His once immaculate white suit was badly torn and black with soot. Bruised, badly mangled, and seriously burned, he was carried on a stretcher to the house on the hill.

In the midst of all the horrible injuries, there were two miraculous escapes from death. A minute or two before the explosion Joe Pittman had decided the fourteen foot engine flywheel needed oiling. The huge metal wheel had held up the heavy timbers and kept him from being crushed to death. "It was by the grace of God and that big flywheel that my life was spared," he told his wife; and that was the day Joe Pittman became a Christian.

Then there was the experience of one of the stamp mill workers.

"When the explosion came I felt a terrific air suction that seemed to drag me toward the door and before I knew it, I was out in the road. If I lived ten lifetimes, I could never forget today, especially when I took a look at where the engine room and boiler room once stood."

And in the midst of all the confusion there was a mysterious unknown hero, a stranger in a white suit who seemed to be everywhere, directing rescue work, helping individual victims and getting others to the first aid station set up under a tree. By noon when people were saying that someone should thank this Samaritan, he was already gone. Oddly enough, no one knew the fellow or where he had come from . . . nor would anyone ever know.

Outside the Captain's home the people of Kershaw were gathering in groups in the front yard. They talked in low tones or prayed as they waited for good news . . . some encouraging announcement to give them hope, but the Captain never recovered enough to speak or recognize anyone. Attending physicians determined soon that nothing could be done to save him. For thirty-five minutes he had lain crushed by heavy timbers and covered with hot brick and debris . . . forty-year old Ernest Thies never regained consciousness.

From the open pits, from the shafts and tunnels, all the workers gathered around the stamp mill to look at the ruin. Mining activity came to a standstill with everyone congregated next door under the shade of the large oak in the Pittmans' yard. All work in every part of the mine ceased, although, there was no reason to shut down as the destruction of the stamp mill need not have stopped the other mining operations.

For some reason, no attempt was made to clean up the area or salvage any of the machinery. The men seemed in a state of deep shock. From the morning of the explosion and the death of the Captain all everyone did each day was to come and sit under the big oak tree and talk . . . sometimes in almost hushed tones and with attitudes of gloom and despair.

"Sodom and Gomorrah has sunk into the ground and the evil thereof," Frank Pearson would intone nodding his head certain that his prophecy of doom had come to pass. Strangely enough, none of the miners ever went back to work at the Haile Mine again. One moment the mine was reputedly as rich as the Mines of Ophir and the next, it was rubble.

Captain Thies had never appointed an assistant and all decisions had been made by him. He was the sole supervisory link with the company. Now, there was no communication . . . no leader . . . no one who knew what to do. The Captain's life and that of the Haile seemed to end simultaneously, almost as if there was some mystical union between the man and the mine. . . .

It was years later before mining began again productively at the Haile, the mine once said to be the largest producer of gold on the eastern seaboard. The Charlotte-based Piedmont Mining Company began operations in 1980 and since then has produced more than twenty-five thousand ounces of gold and twelve thousand ounces of silver from the seven acre site.

10.
The Discovery of Gold in Georgia

The gold had lain there since nature sculpted the Appalachians, filling crevices, secreted in the pockets where metallic gas had formed and cooled within the molten rock to form the miraculous yellow metal. And above it the Cherokee Indians lived for generations—planting, hunting, and fishing—innocent of the treasure beneath their feet for which men would kill and die.

In 1540 Hernando de Soto and his explorers were the first white men the Indians of the Georgia mountains had ever seen. Although the gold they sought was here, the disappointed Spaniards did not find it and it would lie undisturbed for three more centuries.

They had no interest in the fact that they had brought a primitive people from the stone age into the age of metal as swiftly and unexpectedly as a flash of lightning strikes a tree in the forest.

The Cherokees watched Spanish axes of iron and steel felling a great tree in an hour while stone axes shattered and the task might take them several days. Spanish knives transformed game into food or pelts with magical speed as Indian hunters looked on in amazement. Their lives would never be the same.

In the late 1700s European settlers began to arrive and the Cherokees adapted rapidly to the civilization of their new white neighbors. Sequoya, a Cherokee scholar, invented the symbols for an alphabet and many soon learned to read their own newspaper edited by the articulate, intelligent Elias Boudinot. They lived in houses, some modest, some elaborate, and farmed, raised cattle, and owned slaves. The Cherokees began to dress like the whites, absorbed their customs, and adopted the Christian religion. Ironically, many of the very Christians who were so concerned over the state of their souls were to seize their land and belongings and exile them, for the discovery of gold changed the white settlers and their Indian friends into adversaries.

How did it all start and who was first to discover gold in Georgia? It is believed to have been a North Carolinian named Parks. The Parks family moved to Georgia in 1818, buying farmland at the edge of a forest not far from the site where the Dahlonega Court House would one day be built. Benny Parks was deer hunting in the winter of 1828 when he tripped on a stone and almost fell.

"My toe hurt so dad-blamed bad I picked up that rock and was ready to pitch it," the old Georgia farmer said, as he reportedly told the story in 1894. "But something stopped me . . . it just didn't feel like an ordinary rock. When I looked at it closer, it glinted. It glinted like gold and doggone . . . it really was!" Since he came from North Carolina where the gold rush began some years before, Parks was not surprised. White haired with sparking blue eyes, Benny Parks had a superior memory even at 94; and he seldom stumbled over a word as he described to a reporter the events that followed his discovery.

"The land I wanted belonged to Reverend Mr. Obarr, who, though a preacher was a hard man and desperate. I went to him and told him that I thought I could find gold on his place, if he would give me a lease. He laughed as though he did not believe me, and consented. So, a lease for forty years was written out, the consideration of which was, that I was to give him one-fourth of the gold mined. I took into partnership a friend, in whom I had confidence ... went over to the spot with a pan and turning over some earth, it looked like the yellow of an egg. It was more than my eyes could believe!

"The news got abroad and such excitement you never saw. It seemed within a few days as if the whole earth must have heard of it; for men descended upon the area from every state. . . . They came afoot, on horseback ... in wagons, acting more like crazy men than anything else. All the way from where Dahlonega now stands ... it was all forest then ... to Nuckollsville, there were men panning in the streams and digging holes in the hillsides.

"The saddest man in that county was Preacher Obarr from whom I had leased the land. He thought the lease was a joke but now he found out that it was in earnest. One day he approached me brusquely saying, 'Mr. Parks, I want your lease.' 'But I will not sell it to you,' I replied. 'Why not?" he asked. 'Well,' I answered, 'even if I were willing, it is now out of my power; for I have taken a partner, and I know he would never consent to it. I have given him my word and I will keep it.' 'You will suffer for this, yet,' said Obarr menacingly.

"Two weeks later I saw a party of two men and two women approaching. I knew it was Obarr's family, intent upon trouble. Knowing Obarr's fondness for litigation, I warned my men to hold their own but to take no offensive step. 'Mr. Parks,' were the minister's first words, 'I want the mine.' 'If you were to pay me ten times its value,' I replied, 'I would not sell it to you.' 'Well, the longest pole will knock off the persimmon,' he said threateningly.

"At that moment Mrs. Obarr broke the sluice-gates. Water ran through a sluice in which gold was panned in order to wash away mud and substances lighter than gold.

The water was kept in the sluice by a gate. A worker was in the ditch and the woman threw rocks in the water in order to splash him. Failing to make him aggressive, she burst into tears. When her son advanced to attack him, I seized him by the collar and flung him back. Then the party went off, swore out warrants against us, and had us all arrested. All this was done for intimidation but it failed to work . . . and then I lost a fortune.

"Senator Calhoun wanted to buy my lease and I sold it for what I thought was a good price. The very first month after the sale, he took out 24,000 pennyweights of gold [1.555 grams equals a pennyweight and 31.1 grams equals an ounce]. Then I was inclined to be mad with him as Obarr had been with me. But that is the peculiarity of gold-mining. You will go, day after day, exhausting your means and your strength, until you give up. Then, the first man who touches the spot where you have been working finds the gold the first opening he makes. It is just like gambling—all luck."

Parks firmly believed that he was the first discoverer of gold in Georgia. But the Parks strike was quickly followed by more.

In 1829 gold was discovered almost simultaneously in White County's Nacoochee Valley and numerous places in north Georgia. Many of the placer deposits of the Dahlonega and Nacoochee Valley area, occurring along small branches and creeks, were rich and easily worked. Miners with picks followed the discoveries and from these two centers mining spread elsewhere.

The news got abroad and with it there was great excitement. "It seemed that in a few days the whole world must have heard of it for men came from every state. They came afoot, they came on horseback and in wagons acting more

Bucket shafts like this were used in many mines after placer gold played out.
(North Carolina Department of Archives and History Photo)   *Harper's New Monthly Magazine, 1857*

like crazy men than anything else," wrote one newspaper reporter. The "crazy men" settled on a ridge between two gold bearing streams, the Etowah and the Chastatee which was the boundary of Cherokee Territory.

The rush to the mines brought in thousands of adventurers to seek their fortune and with them came gamblers and swindlers to cheat them out of what they found. Auraria was Georgia's first boomtown with five taverns, a hundred houses, eighteen or twenty stores, a dozen law offices, and a newspaper. For the first few years the gold came from the gravel of stream beds which in the southeast was called deposit mining but in California it was known as placer or gulch mining. Although the process was crude and simple, the best data estimate that the mines yielded from sixteen to twenty million dollars in the ten years between 1829 and 1839.

When the first gold nugget was found the Indians paid little attention. They had never understood why the white men, beginning with de Soto, were always looking for this yellow metal.

The Cherokees never really expected the brutal act that would send them away from the mountains they loved, for they reckoned without the determination of gold-lusting Georgians and President Andrew Jackson who was an old Indian fighter. Even then it probably could not have happened if as early as 1802 the federal government had not promised to remove the Cherokee Indians from Georgia in return for the state giving up all land claims in Alabama and Mississippi. Whites and Indians were coexisting peacefully until the discovery was made that their land had gold on it. Even if Jackson's sympathies had been with the Cherokees, Georgia was an independent state and able to defy the government in Washington.

Prospectors invaded the Indian lands driving Cherokee families from their homes, stealing food, and killing their cattle. Men who tried to protect their families were beaten and some even killed by the gold crazed miners.

Cherokee Chief, John Ross, appealed to the president for help. He sought to close the gold camps on Indian land and to protect the Indians from robbery and murder with soldiers, if necessary, but Andrew Jackson sent so few troops he might as well have sent none. Seeing this, the governor of Georgia realized President Jackson would not stop him and he took advantage of the opportunity to send the state militia onto Cherokee land to drive out the Indians.

Even the Supreme Court ruled in favor of the Indians but the President flouted the law and allowed them to be forced off their land.

"If I had known this would happen, I would have killed Jackson at the Battle of Horseshoe Bend," responded old Chief Junaluska bitterly. Years before the chief had fought at Jackson's side helping him defeat hostile Creek Indians. Now he had been betrayed by the man he had aided.

A handful of Georgians sympathized with the Cherokees but the majority were determined to seize their land, right or wrong, and these people were more powerful than the friends of the Indians.

Troops are not the only way to harass citizenry. Georgia decided to use the law, also, as a means to oppress and steal; and the state legislature passed law after law designed to discriminate against the Cherokee and make their lives intolerable. The worst law was to prohibit the Indians, who had lived there for centuries, from even owning land in Georgia.

In 1832 the land that the state had seized from the Cherokees was distributed to white Georgians through a land lottery. In order to qualify for lottery tickets citizens had to be either heads of families, or widows or orphans of Revolutionary soldiers. Over four million acres of Cherokee land was given away in the lottery held at the state capitol in Milledgeville; and those fortunate enough to win a lot paid just an eighteen dollar fee to claim forty acres of land.

Excitement among the white citizens was tremendous as day after day men stood outside the lottery office awaiting the results of the drawings, especially for lots like number 1031 and 1052 in District Twelve. These lots were in gold rich Auraria and Dahlonega, part of Lumpkin County, and were valued at one hundred thousand dollars each.

When the lottery was over state troops arrived in Dahlonega; and General Winfield Scott, who headquartered near Auraria, began rounding up the Indians for the trip west. It would be a sad and brutal chapter in American history. Troops forced entire Cherokee families at gunpoint to leave their homes with only the belongings they were able to carry with them.

Whether old people or children, strong or weak, they were ordered to walk mile after mile west across five states to Oklahoma. Few families survived intact, for the harsh weather killed many along the way. Accusations of cruelty on the part of the soldiers abounded and although some were exaggerated many were probably true.

Soon thirty-five to forty-thousand men were working in the Georgia mines. They were a rough living, tough fighting crew, with Georgians fighting Tennesseans and Carolinians over ownership of gold deposits. One such bloody battle gave the stream of Battle Branch its name. A prospector was mortally wounded with a blow from a spade and several others badly hurt when sixty Carolinians attacked twenty

Georgians. The Georgians fought fiercely, drove them off, and retained possession of the mine.

Infamous outlaws such as Munro, Tracy, and Dexter attacked and preyed upon the small mining camps and the more isolated and helpless miners. With the sudden boom in population it was difficult to enforce the law.

Along with miners from Georgia and other southern states large numbers of foreign laborers and some skilled mining engineers with practical experience in European and South American mines had arrived. On the streets of Dahlonega, Auraria, and other rural Georgia towns men spoke German, Swiss, Swedish, Spanish, English, Irish, Welsh, and Scottish.

William Gilmore Simms gives a most romantic account of the Dahlonega gold belt in his contemporary novel, *Guy Rivers: A Tale of Georgia*. But in reality, life in the gold fields was brutal and hard. Food was scarce and expensive, for the number of farmers had never been great and now some of them were mining rather than growing food for market. At the height of the gold rush a letter from an Aurarian to a friend in Augusta states that there was not one pound of bacon for sale in Lumpkin County. Even with drovers herding constant streams of swine, cattle, and fowl to be slaughtered in the gold country, meat was still in short supply.

After every rain, men were in the stream beds panning gold that had washed down from the mountains and at night there was merrymaking and quarreling around camp fires. They often gambled away their day's gold find with cards and dice or squandered it on whiskey.

Gold dust was so common, a miner might pay with loose gold from his vest pocket and the price of a drink was the dust that lay on the point of his knife. Miners purchased their supplies with "wash grains" or from the gold dust they carried in goose quills weighing it out on small hand scales. They also used gold dust at the many banks, stores, hotels, and taverns mushrooming beside the roads to the mining towns.

The Cherokee Hotel was advertised as being "in the center of the gold region where one can get maps and diagrams" and Traveler's Home boasted "a house of entertainment, writing rooms, the best food the country furnishes, a bar with choice liquors and stables with horses." Also popular were the Planter's Hotel in Gainesville; the Allatooney, the Etowah, the Golden Egg, and the well-known Ma Paschal's House in Auraria; and six miles southwest of Dahlonega, the Habersham, the Chestatee, the Nacoochee, and the Choestoes.

Gold speculation was rampant with the newspapers full of ads for mines for sale and the turnover on mines so rapid it was almost impossible to keep up with the ownership of many of them. Lot No. 747 which belonged to Martin Strother in 1832 passed through the hands of at least eighteen other owners before it was acquired by the Yahoola and Cane Creek Hose Mining Company less than thirty years later.

Many buyers were adventurers who put all their money into land and left nothing for operating costs. Other miners worked singly or in small groups and jumped from place to place as new discoveries were made. There were few experienced mining operators or engineers.

These were chaotic, uncertain times—often when banks sent agents out to the mining camps to buy gold the agents themselves caught gold fever, became prospectors, and never returned! Some mining companies acted as banks, buying gold and issuing their own paper money which circulated freely. State newspapers carried exchange rates

The experienced Georgia miners used the "long tom" and took their invention West with them.
Harper's New Monthly Magazine, 1857

on gold from the various mines in the same column with stock and bank notes.

Noted geologist, William P. Blake, estimated that only one-third of the extensive Georgia deposits were touched, and probably not more than half of that recovered, so, it is probable there is much gold still below ground at the early mine sites.

Why did so much gold go unrecovered not only in Georgia but in all of the southeastern mines? One reason was that tools for working placer deposits were incredibly inefficient. Miners used picks, axes, pans, crude longtoms, splint baskets, and gumlog rockers—hardly a technological approach.

Later a combined cradle and rocker was patented by General Thomas Jefferson Green of Warrenton, North Carolina, and worked by miners in the Carolinas and Virginia. Flat boats were used to dredge up dirt from the river bottoms and John C. Calhoun even rigged up a steamboat with a diving bell attached.

When the miners discovered deposits on ridges away from the streams they were faced with new difficulties, for not only did they have to dig the gravel and pound the larger stones, but they also had to cart it to streams for washing. Opening of ridge and vein mines called for expensive machinery with which to crush the ore and extract gold. Then came the forges, furnaces, stamp mills, pumps, engines, and Mexican arastras with steam and water power to drive them . . . still inefficient by modern standards.

Quicksilver came into use to collect gold from the crushed ore and by 1833 McDuffie County had the first water driven stamp mill in the United States. Day after day its noise could be heard as the hard quartz was crushed into ore. In the 1830s capital began to flow in from the northeastern financial centers and Europe and was invested in the Georgia mines.

Like the Carolinians, many Georgia planters ran their mines throughout the year as a sideline to their plantation crops. These men had the temperament of farmers, not gold hunters, and little interest in engineering and mining technology. When the price of cotton was high they deserted the mines for the fields and when cotton prices were low, they flocked to the mines.

Thomas Lumsden, a planter from Nacoochee, took his slaves to the mines between the growing and harvesting seasons. His records show that one winter his slaves removed thirty-thousand dollars worth of gold. This still did not inspire Lumsden to concentrate on gold. There always seemed to be plenty more to find, for in the early days each rain brought fresh gold down from the mountains and into the streams.

For a long time a local mint had been needed. Since the trip to Philadelphia was dangerous and miners were often robbed on the way, many a southern prospecter breathed a sigh of relief when the Dahlonega Mint opened its doors in 1838. Before the mint closed at the time of the Civil War it had made over six million dollars worth of gold coins.

Georgia gold was assayed as the finest in the United States, some running as high as .996 fine with the average being about .950. Unlike the 28 pound nuggets found in North Carolina and a 161 pound nugget found in California, the largest found in Georgia weighed only 4½ pounds . . . yet there was talk of nuggets so large they had to be broken up before the finder could carry them! Many, undoubtedly, went unrecorded.

West of Dahlonega in the old village cemetery there were several rich little veins that showed gold freely and often when graves were dug enticing specimens of quartz sprinkled over with gold were exposed to view. This could be the ultimate distraction to a miner looking down decorously into an open grave trying to listen to the service. But at least they had the assurance that their comrade was being laid to rest in a tomb where the walls glittered with the yellow metal for which the deceased had toiled his life away.

Then in 1849 came exciting news. Gold was discovered in California and scores of Georgians left their diggings to go West since the rich placer gold in the Georgia deposits had long since been worked out. Large profits could now be made only by mechanizing and investing substantial amounts of money. Despite the pleas of Dr. Stephenson for the miners to stay and his oft quoted words . . . that there was still gold in those hills . . . and after production of over fifty million dollars worth of gold, by 1850 the Georgia mines were abandoned.

The Georgians took with them an invention from the southern gold fields called the longtom which had not yet been used in California. The longtom was simply a trough of boards about twelve feet long and eight inches deep with an opening at the head a foot wide and the trough increased in width gradually until it was about two feet wide at the lower end. At this lower end was a piece of sheet iron with holes that the finer sand fell through leaving the larger rocks to wash out. This allowed a man to work many, many times the gravel he could have panned or worked with a rocker.

The more venturesome miners went West to the new El Dorado. A news item in 1852 mentioned thirty Georgians on one vessel who died on their way to Panama and California and five of them were from Lumpkin County.

Others who headed West and got there were the Russell brothers, John Gregory, Lewis Ralston, William Anderson, Joseph McAfee, Solomon Roe, Samuel Bates, John Hampton, William G. Smith, E. G. Miller, George W. Parks, Carter Pratt, J. W. Samuel and many more whose names went unrecorded.

11.
"Free Jim"

It was 1830 and the men streaming into north Georgia were the rowdiest, lustiest rogues imaginable. Many of the wagons were headed toward Pigeon Roost where gold had first been discovered and the clouds of dust raised by the wheels and horses hoofs left a gritty clay coating on Jim Boisclair's face as he walked along the road.

He strode on unheeding and even as he knew the journey meant a fresh start his heart was heavy over leaving Augusta.

He assisted a South Carolina miner with his horses at one of the watering places and the man offered him a ride—"If ye'll wash your face so's I can tell what ye look like," and Jim gladly complied. Jake Clay who was only a few years older had worked at the Brewer Mine and was now on his way to Dahlonega.

Jim was both excited and apprehensive as he heard him talk about gold for he knew he had a problem his companion did not have . . . an obstacle that had defeated many good men. It was not lack of determination or courage or even money for he had enough gold coins sewn in his clothing to buy more than one claim.

Upon reaching Dahlonega he found a general store where the owner was glad to rent an unused storage room and despite that fact that the occupation sometimes seemed menial to him, he opened a small pastry shop using the skills he had acquired as a boy working for a baker in Augusta. Tall, well built, with black curly hair, amazing bright blue eyes and skin that appeared to be tanned a golden hue by the sun, Jim Boisclair was a man that people in Dahlonega looked at twice.

He was quick to ingratiate himself with his customers and his shop became popular with many of the town's most prominent citizens. One was Dr. J. J. Singleton, Superintendent of the new U.S. Mint who often dropped by in the afternoon to talk and Jim listened attentively. But he absorbed even more eagerly the stories of Duncan, a part Indian miner whom the townfolk regarded with superstitious awe.

Duncan had dreams that helped him pinpoint the location of gold and it was he who later discovered the rich Findley vein. Eager as he was to do so Jim could not buy a claim of his own and herein lay his major obstacle to complete social acceptance and fortune—Jim Boisclair was part black. Whether quadroon or octaroon it didn't matter, according to Georgia law no one with black heritage could either buy or sell property. He often asked himself of what use was money if it could not buy property?

"I wonder how many slaves old John Calhoun's got working in his mine down near the Chestatee River," speculated Duncan as they talked one day in the bake shop. "From the number I see coming into the store next door, I'd say at least a dozen," replied Jim. He sometimes looked at them and thought how much better off he was than they despite his own problem and, perhaps, that could yet be resolved. Duncan, his part Indian friend, was considered white. If he could find a mine site for sale he believed he could persuade Duncan to purchase it for him and one afternoon when Dr. Singleton was in the shop he asked if he knew of a good mine for sale.

"I think I can find one for you. There's gold on most of the lots, not just near the Calhoun Mine and Briarpatch mines, and I'm convinced there is a rich vein that extends beneath my mine and the Yahoola."

Mine sites had been distributed by lottery to Revolutionary soldiers, heads of families, widows and orphans as long as they were white. Occasionally these individuals might sell their claim and a week later Singleton came in to tell him of just such an opportunity. He took his glasses off and leaned toward Jim across the counter so that the full impact of his announcement would sink in.

"I've found the right mine site for you, Jim. It belongs to an orphan and her guardian is disposed to sell."

"Where is it," said Jim, his heart beginning to pound.

"Only a short distance and between two of the richest claims in Lumpkin County."

Luckily, Duncan approved the claim and arranged its purchase. Jim sunk two shafts and before long the mine was turning a healthy profit, so with his friend's help once more, he purchased a building and opened the largest general store in Dahlonega. Each day it was crowded with gold miners buying cooking utensils, cutlery, padlocks, clothing, food, brandy, and imported delicacies.

One morning he was passing the courthouse when he heard the sing-song voice of an auctioneer and the murmur of voices. It was a slave auction. Repugnant as they had always been to him, he was somehow drawn to it and he paused to watch.

"Here's a pretty little wench. I'll open the bid for her at two hundred," said the auctioneer.

"How 'bout two hundred and fifty," a man's voice spoke up.

"Can't let her go for that . . . who'll make it three hundred, three . . ."

"Three hundred," said someone.

Singleton was standing looking on curiously and Jim had just reached his side when for the first time he saw the girl on the block. She held up her head haughtily and her eyes stared straight ahead as if she did not see the crowd. Exquisitely beautiful, he judged her to be a quadroon for her skin was the color of the pale amber sugar he sold in his store. Like his own skin, it occurred to him.

He heard her voice and the intonation of the words were a shock. Once more he was hearing his mother speak to him in a language the old woman had never forgotten . . . the soft patois she had spoken from the time of her birth in Haiti. As he listened he realized this beautiful woman was pleading eloquently for her freedom in Haitian French. It was a fervent, eloquent plea . . . she had never been a slave.

He saw the skirt of red negro cloth given to slaves, the cheap, rough fabric against her beautiful creamy skin . . . she was a Creole girl. Although free when they arrived in the seaports many were seized by unscrupulous traders and sold into slavery.

The burden was upon these poor people, who often could not even speak English, to prove they were free and not escaped slaves. If they could not they were put in chains, placed upon the block and sold as slaves. Even Jim himself could be at risk if he were in one of the port cities or traveling in a slave state where he was unknown.

"Singleton, that girl has never been a slave. She is a Dominican or Haitian who has somehow gotten into the clutches of slavers."

"I doubt we can prove it. Do you want me to bid on her for you?"

"Yes," replied Jim without hesitation. His decisiveness was characteristic and one of his best qualities but sometimes it placed him in danger. Singleton raised a finger.

"Three hundred and fifty dollars."

"By golly! I'll make it four hundred!"

Jim turned to see the bidder who appeared to be a thoroughly inebriated drover ... probably just come in from driving animals along the trail that led through Dahlonega from Tennessee. On his head was a dusty, battered round-brim hat and he wore a filthy tan shirt with sleeves rolled to the elbow revealing tremendous hairy arms. He may run up the bid with no money and no idea of what he's doing thought Jim.

"Four hundred," he heard Singleton's firm voice bid. And then came a noisy belch capped with a hiccup. "Unnhhhh," the drunk swayed backward, was caught by someone and leaned up against a tree. The auctioneer stared over at him expectantly waiting for another bid. His eyelids closed, his unshaven chin drooped forward upon his soiled homespun shirt and his lips hung loose and flaccid, like tobacco-stained slabs of country ham. No bid came.

Staring around at the crowd the auctioneer began to cajole.

"Come on folks, Who will give me four-fifty for this purty thing." Jim hated to look at the girl whose face held both terror and shame at her nakedness.

"Do I hear four hundred and fifty? One of you fine gentlemen better speak up!" At this the man sitting against the tree stirred and opened his eyes. He tried to speak but could not get out a coherent bid. Jim wiped his forehead with his handkerchief.

"Going, going, gone! Sold to Dr. J. J. Singleton for four hundred dollars. You've got a prize here, sir." Jim handed Singleton a quill full of gold dust and while it was being weighed he gave the girl his coat. Once covered she held herself proudly but there was fear in her eyes. Her name was Desiree Radeau. Jim thanked Singleton and led Desiree to his store a short distance away.

He found proper undergarments and a blouse for her but could not persuade her to take any more clothes nor would she look at him. From what she said, he saw she believed he had bought her to be his slave! Only after she understood that she was to have her freedom did she happily select two skirts, several blouses, and some shoes.

She regarded with distaste the rough homespun petticoats and skirts which were all most of the miners' wives and daughters were accustomed to wearing. Desiree went through everything like an impatient child and eventually found a soft petticoat which she held against her face smiling and stroking it to show him how soft it was. Where would she stay he wondered and then he thought of his friends, Jake and Jennie Clay. Jake had a big heart and he and Jim had long been friends. He had no slaves and with two white helpers he worked his own mine while Jim, too, employed only free labor.

Jake and Jennie were agreeable to Desiree boarding with them, and in return Desiree taught Jennie French. Both of their mines were producing well and the early 1840s saw the entire town booming. In the winter when John C. Calhoun's slaves were through with the crops, the days were shorter, and they would come into the store to pick up supplies.

"He's striking it mighty rich out there," was sometimes heard and Jake would mutter about people who had slaves to dig their gold out of the ground and how he sure would hate to trade with them.

"What can I do? Refuse to sell to him, Jake. That would just be foolishness. He would only go elsewhere." But inwardly he was often angry over the treatment sometimes visited on a slave and he didn't lose sleep over runaways. His own miners were either white or free blacks and in the mines the races worked side by side.

One day in the store a woman's voice spoke up from behind him.

"Free Jim! Remember me?"

It was a shock to be called "Free Jim" for it brought back the days in Augusta and here people just called him Jim. He turned to look into the cruel, golden eyes of a young mulatto woman.

"Don't you remember me? I'm Angelique, Mambo's granddaughter."

He did and his reaction to the memory was not a pleasant one. It was from Angelique that he had first learned about the dark magic of voodoo and since then he had always found ways to avoid her. He was not sure he believed that she had any real power but about her he had always felt a pervasive aura of evil.

"You're a big man here in Dahlonega aren't you?" Your mama know how good you're doing?"

"She's up here living with me."

"And Mr. Michael? Lordy, if he could just see his ... see you now. It was him tole you to get out of Augusta, warn't it, Jim?"

Jim felt the hot blood surge to his face and it was all he could do to keep from leaping over the counter and choking this woman. He turned to arrange the stock on the shelves behind him and as he did all the terrible hurt and anger of the past began to boil up within him toward the man who was his father ... who was white ... who would never be proud of him ... who didn't even want to own him as his son. Once more he felt torn asunder by the agony he had suffered during his boyhood in Augusta.

Until then he had not realized how seldom Michael Boisclair had occupied his thoughts during the past few years here in Dahlonega. He had become someone new and now here was Angelique reopening the deepest wound of his life.

"If you need me to work for you in the store, my husband and I are livin' over at Auraria. Miz Paschal can tell you where I am."

"I don't need any help at present, Angelique," he said stiffly.

"Why, Jim. Don't ya think you and Henry and me oughta get together for old times?" He was enveloped in waves of nausea and anger and replied harshly.

"No! I don't."

"Well! Free Jim's gotten too high and mighty to have anything to do with his old Augusta friends. Let's go, Henry," she said to her husband who had joined her. The ingratiating expression left her face and her eyes turned wintry; and she was right in the sense that he wanted to put the years in Augusta behind him . . . repudiate the past and the pain of those years forever.

He was grateful to see his old friend, William Thomas, entering the store. Thomas, a merchant also, was known for the influence he once had with the Cherokees. He was traveling through the area and their talk helped Jim forget the dark, hateful miasma of his encounter with Angelique. The two men went over to Jake Clay's house and Thomas soon saw that Jim was enthralled by Desiree, for this, rather than his miner friend's conversation, was the magnet that drew him so often.

They were married in 1845 and the wedding was a topic of conversation for months afterward. Nothing had ever been seen in Dahlonega to approach Desiree's magnificent dress imported by Jim from France. At the reception only the finest brandy was served and many a rough miner rubbed shoulders with the elite of Lumpkin County. Perhaps, not in Augusta or Savannah, but in the frontier atmosphere of north Georgia, money was the great equalizer and Jim had it.

He and Desiree made trips to Augusta to select materials for the house they were building and Jim was investigating business interests. He was much impressed with the canal work and how its completion would bring factories to the area. Cotton boats already using it were tied up at busy wharves. They bought their doors and windows at the Augusta Manufacturing Company. The opening of the canal was to bring the dawn of a new day in Georgia.

Three years passed and Desiree was pregnant. Jim was overjoyed. Jennie Clay began sewing furiously. Scarcely a day passed that some article of furniture for the baby's room or a bolt of fine batiste for gowns did not arrive at the store.

One morning an excited Jake Clay burst into Jim's office.

"Jim. Have you heard the news?" They've discovered gold in California and everybody's going."

"Going to California? What's the sense of that? There's plenty of gold right here in Lumpkin County." And that is what Dr. M. F. Stephenson said to two hundred miners in an impassioned plea from the courthouse steps a short time later. Pointing to Findley Ridge a half mile to the south he exclaimed, "Why go to California. In that ridge lies more gold than man ever dreamt of. There's millions in it." But by 1848 the rich placer deposits had been worked out and fortunes could no longer be made with the old pick and shovel methods.

Stories were heard from the West of "new diggings" . . . diggings where old miners and pioneer methods were rewarded by showers of gold. The exodus began and despite his longing to go, Jim resisted it. Then he hit upon a great idea.

Many miners couldn't afford to go. He would pay their way and they could pay him back with half their gold from the first year. It was a handpicked group with the exception of Henry, Angelique's husband, who had begged to go. Maybe the man wasn't so bad . . . maybe it was only Angelique.

Whenever he saw Angelique her eyes smoldered with hostility. Once he asked her where she had been living before she came to Dahlonega and his worst intuitions were confirmed when she said New Orleans. He had heard about the voodoo rituals held on the shore of Lake Pontchartrain and he had also heard from Mrs. Paschal that the woman had made few friends in Auraria.

A baby girl was born to Desiree and Jim and he could not have been a more loving father. When he returned from the store in the evening the child, whom they had named Delight, was his first concern. The days and months sped by and in a way he began to dread the trip he would have to make to California to recover his investment; but go he would and when he was honest with himself he knew it was because he was fully as eager as the miners he had staked.

Jim stared from the dock at a ship that listed to one side, most of it submerged, and any seamen aboard long since off to the gold fields. Like many others of all sizes and descriptions it lay abandoned in the San Francisco Harbor. The vessels looked like toys that giants had tired of and carelessly pitched into the water. When gold fever struck crews all responsibility was forgotten.

He thought how abnormal it was for a captain to quit his ship, a pharmacist to simply lock his front door and never return, a doctor abandon his practice, and all sorts of individuals to forget home, family, and occupation. But he had seen it happen when men dreamt of enormous wealth and recalled one man after another closing up his business and leaving Dahlonega for the gold fields.

Those who could afford it booked passage on sailing ships around Cape Horn to San Francisco, roughly an eighteen thousand mile trip, others took a short cut through the isthmus of Panama desperately combating mosquitoes and disease.

And then there were those he himself had staked, miners who otherwise would have been unable to afford the trip. Most went overland completely ignorant of the distance or hardship setting out upon the trails that led west from St. Joe, Independence, and other cities along the Missouri.

He thought about his wife and baby with a sense of guilt. After all, if he had not had to collect his return on the stakes he had given the Georgia men he might never have gone West. But in all honesty, hé knew that wasn't true; he was going because like many of the others, he loved adventure and it had been years since he'd had a taste of it.

He heard some of the men had fought for places on the boat but gradually everyone became more orderly and waited their turn which was often two weeks; and when they had traveled beyond the Missouri Valley they suffered for the spring and summer of 1849 was a cold, wet time. People were miserable and the killer cholera raged with such ferocity that many were buried before they ever set eyes on the high plains.

He would never forget riding across those endless plains himself, staring ahead day after day for hundreds of miles at the barrier of the Rockies and the snow-capped peaks. And, beyond the hardships of the Rockies came a long trek through the desert with no trails and no water. And when his resolve was beginning to flag he found the trail to El Dorado barred by the steep Sierras.

Sometimes he thought that he would like to have been with a group like the Jayhawkers who traveled with no women or children . . . a tough, self-sufficient breed, who made the best time of all getting across country to the gold fields. The would-be prospectors Jim had joined were store-keepers, bank clerks and farmers save for a professional gambler and two former military men named James McDuffy and Thomas Rice.

It was with the latter that he had the most in common; and after the officers surprise at meeting a light-skinned man of black heritage who obviously had both brains and money the three became fast friends and the acknowledged leaders of the group. Jim talked with them about the miners from the Dahlonega area whom he had loaned money.

"They're reliable fellows I've known for years," and then he hesitated, "except for a couple of them and with them, well, I'll wait and see."

As for the gambler in their group, Jim knew his kind from the saloons back in Dahlonega and Auraria and he tolerated him.

In turn Jack Gamble paid Jim grudging respect and was more apt to do some piece of work when he asked him than when the military men did. He seemed to take pleasure in ignoring what he called insolently their "orders from headquarters." Jim regarded him warily for he knew men like Gamble were as quick with a pistol as with a card especially away from any town or semblance of law. Gamble was the first to leave the group when they finally arrived in San Francisco.

He and his two friends were astonished to discover how hard it was to find decent lodgings and they felt fortunate to obtain a room in the former clipper ship *Niantic*. The vessel had sunk in shallow water but earth had been filled in around it and the ship had become a hostelry.

Jim went around for a day with Rice and McDuffy while they shopped for picks and other supplies to take prospecting with them, giving them advice out of his own mining experience on what to purchase. The three were good friends by now and he realized that he hated to see them go. Rice had decided to head for Hangtown and McDuffy for Marysville. They would see what luck they had prospecting on their own for a while and then they planned to meet in Grass Valley.

"We may run into some of those miners from Georgia," said McDuffy, "and if we do, we'll tell them you're out here, Jim."

"Fine, I'm going to look around here first and then start the rounds of the camps. Those fellows are probably all over the place."

They had dinner together that night at the Niantic Hotel and the next morning his two friends left at daybreak. Free Jim found San Francisco an amazing city. The streets were neither paved nor graded. The mud at Clay and Kearny streets in the heart of town was so deep that the sign which said, *This street is impassable—not even jackassable* made Jim grin. He stared curiously at houses on the same street that were twenty to fifty feet higher or lower than their neighbors'.

"Hello, stranger. How's diggin's? Jim went from one gold camp to another.
Harper's New Monthly Magazine, 1858

Since he had paid for a month in advance at the Niantic, Jim decided to begin by checking lodging houses with the idea that some of the Georgians might be waiting for a ship back home. He was shocked at the conditions in them—rats the size of a terrier, noxious bugs and after three days of having his senses revolted he still had not found any men from Georgia.

He was ravenous for fresh vegetables for despite the enormous yield of nearby farms and a fine climate that produced carrots a yard long and cabbages twenty inches in diameter, vegetables were a luxury only the very rich could afford. A quart of good whiskey cost thirty dollars but Jim was a light drinker and the exorbitant price did not inconvenience him.

On the fourth day at one of the lodging houses, he heard a familiar name . . . that of Jeremy Green. "He come back from the gold fields and I could tell right away, he'd struck it rich," said the proprietress. "Sure enough, next I heard, Mr. Green had bought himself a share in the El Dorado."

When Jim walked through the swinging doors of the gambling house and saloon the two men recognized each other instantly and Green came out from behind the bar and gave him a bear hug.

"Jim! Well dad-blame it! When did you get here?"

"About a week ago. I'm glad to see you've done well for yourself, Jeremy." He looked around at the large, square room of rough boards and its elegant furnishings. A painting of a nude woman covered the wall above the bar, extending the length of it; at one end of the room was a raised platform from which an orchestra blared and at the other end was a bar with large mirrors of fine cut glass behind it.

"Come over here. I want you to have a drink on the house. Jerry Thomas will make you one of his famous 'Tom and Jerry's,' won't you Professor Thomas." The professor nodded and grinned and adeptly began to pour and shake and pour again.

"Yeah, I made out pretty good, Jim, and I owe you for givin' me a chance to come our here. I want to pay you the money right now for my passage and half 'a my first year's earnin's." Jim nodded. He had loaned Jeremy money several times back home and never doubted that he could trust him.

"Now, sit down over here with your drink and I've ordered some oysters for you—also on the house," he said proudly disappearing for a few minutes.

Throughout the room were gaming tables and upon them huge piles of gold dust, nuggets, and gold and silver coins. There was monte, faro, rondo, roulette, rouge et noir and vingt-et-un. Poker was too slow for the impatient miners who wouldn't sit still long enough to play it and wanted to stake everything upon the spin of the wheel or the turn of a single card.

Jim disliked gambling places, having no interest in gambling himself. He had been around it enough. Nor was it the warnings preached from the pulpit of the little Baptist church back home that bothered him now, it was a certain suppressed violence in this room that he had seldom felt at Dahlonega.

Behind each table sat the dealer in the traditional black and white of the professional gambler. By coincidence, only a few feet away from him at the first table was his acquaintance from the trip West . . . Jack Gamble. Gamble saw him, grinned and gave a mock military salute before returning to his game. While Jim was eating, Jeremy came back grinning, tossed a pouch of gold dust proudly on the table, and pulled up a chair.

"Those Dahlonega boys sure scattered, Jim. I headed for Sacramento myself and then drifted from camp to camp starting at Sutter Creek and working my way south. They say the northern mines is the richest and if I was you, I believe I'd begin lookin' for the Georgia men up around Weaverville and work my way down through the camps toward Coulterville."

"I thought I'd sail up to Sacramento, spend a few days and from there I can head north, then come back and hit the Mother Lode country to the south."

"That's a start. Lordy, Jim, no tellin' where some 'a them boys is. When the gold plays out they move on, ya know."

"Was it rough for you, Jeremy?"

"You know it! I won't never forget that winter of '49. I said to myself, should I stay up here in these damn Sierras and freeze to death with the freezin' cold and snow comin'?"

"Yeah, you could run clean out of food like the men did at Donner Pass."

"That's right. Well, a lot of the fellows went off figuring to come back. They even left bags of gold in their shacks and nobody didn't bother them. Don't know as you could do that now, but they was pretty honest fellows out here that first year."

"And what did you do?"

"You know me, Jim. I dug myself a cave in a hillside like a bear! I had to scrounge mighty hard for food, but when it come spring, ole Jeremy was first at the diggin's."

"And that's when you hit pay dirt?"

"Bein' there to get a good start and breakin' my back diggin'. I tell you, I'm glad to be in Frisco, Jim. A miner's life is the hardest in the world."

"Looks like you could speak to an old friend, Jim" interrupted a soft, insinuating voice.

He turned his head and for a moment he was back in the past. Standing next to him was Angelique. He knew she had left Dahlonega and assumed she had returned to New Orleans and her voodoo practices. No one had told him she had accompanied her husband West.

"Surprised to see me here, Jim?"

He nodded and his eyes held a cautious expression. "I'm surprised to see any woman, Angelique. I could count the women out here on one hand. Where's Henry?"

She shrugged her shoulders insolently. Her dress was garnet taffeta with a low-cut tight bodice which her bare shoulders rose above ... like some dark and poisonous flower thought Jim.

"How should I know. He was at Red Dog awhile ... then a miner told me he's heard Henry struck it rich at Hangtown. Why? You after your money, Jim?"

A rare flame of anger ignited in his eyes.

"I trust him to pay whatever's due me," he replied levelly. A drunken miner swaggered up and began fondling her shoulder. "Your friend there wants to talk to you, Angelique," Jim said said turning back to Jeremy. She gave him a venomous look and disappeared in the throng of men.

"Yeah, I know. She's got some wildcat in her," said Jeremy placatingly, answering Jim's question before he could ask it, "but she brings in the customers. Her husband's still out at one of the camps and they say he's done well. You paid his way out here, didn't you?" Jim nodded.

"The fellow's a braggart and I'm afraid gold's done got its claws in him bad, Jim," said Jeremy swirling the brandy in his glass. His blue eyes above his steel-rimmed glasses held a warning look.

"I hear what you're saying, Jeremy." Jim unfolded his tall frame and stood up. He was thinner from the trip West than he'd ever been in Dahlonega and when he rose, eyes turned to stare at the handsome, muscular man with the bronze skin and touch of gray in the black hair. His dignity and confidence was evident in the way he held himself and even the way he moved commanded respect.

"If I see any of the others who made the trip from Dahlonega, I'll tell them you're out here, Jim," Jeremy said warmly. "Why don't you move over here to the El Dorado?"

Jim thought a moment and then remembered Angelique. "Thanks, but I won't be in town over another day. You've got a good investment here, Jeremy."

"You're right . . . if it don't get burned up in a fire or tore up by the miners. Good luck and be careful, Jim." Jim thought he detected a note of warning in his voice, not an obvious one but still there . . . as muted as the whisper of acacia leaves.

Outside he noticed the square had three sides occupied by buildings that served the dual purpose of hotels and gambling houses. On the fourth side was an old adobe house and as usual, there stood Preacher William Taylor raving against gambling and its evils while an impetuous crowd of miners swarmed in and out of the dens of iniquity he was reviling. Jim could scarcely hear the preacher above the voices and the thunder of riotous music from the gambling houses.

The El Dorado was one of the most celebrated gambling palaces of all and about the square were clustered others such as the Parker House, Empire, Arcade, Verandah, and the Mazourk. Auraria, Georgia, was never like this even in its wildest days.

After packing to leave the next day for the gold camps Jim decided to take a walk. He knew it might be unwise for it was long past dusk but he was used to taking care of himself and this would be his last look at San Francisco before boarding the boat next day for Sacramento. He couldn't get over this city with its mixture of many races and many kinds of faces on the streets—Mexicans, Japanese, Chinese, French, Indian, even some Creole like his beautiful Desiree. And the country . . . already he loved the rounded contours of the buff-colored hills across the bay, the immense expanses of sky and the water so novel for a land-bound Georgian.

He knew Desiree would like San Francisco, where the two of them would not stand out among the kaleidoscope of colors and racial features, a place where they could make a home in an environment more free from prejudice than Georgia would ever be in his time.

He missed her so greatly that when he lay down to sleep at night, his longing to be in her arms was a dull ache within him. He wrote often but the mails were unreliable and he couldn't even be sure that they always got there. When her letters arrived he eagerly devoured every word seeing behind them Desiree's shining black curls, beautiful high cheekbones with the faint flush beneath the skin and the lights that danced in her dark eyes when she smiled at him. The memorized phrases from her letters were in his mind tonight as he walked.

And then, without a warning a dark shadow from a doorway near the square rushed at him.

The crushing blow of a "slung shot" glanced his shoulder near the base of his neck, a blow that would have landed brutally on the back of his head had he not thrown himself to one side. Despite the pain he turned to strike his assailant, a tall dark figure with a beard and a shapeless felt hat pulled down over his eyes. But the man darted off and was quickly lost in a throng of miners surging toward one of the saloons in the square.

Jim thought there was something familiar about him but as the fast beating of his heart slowed he decided it was unlikely that he knew him. Had he purposely singled him out to rob or would he have attacked anyone who passed at that moment? It was probably the latter for hoodlums and former convicts were common in the city and there were thousands of men in San Francisco with felt hats and dark beards.

He was not ordinarily subject to nightmares but that night he had a dream that left him more shaken afterward than he could remember. It had not been about the attack he had suffered earlier in the evening as he might have expected but was about a woman. When he first waked the identity of the woman who had evoked his nocturnal terror escaped him. Then he remembered ... it was Angelique and those golden eyes of hers blazing with hatred had followed him through the labyrinth of his dream somehow becoming the eyes of every person he met.

It was a week long boat trip to Sacramento and there, following Jeremy's advice, he headed north and from Weaverville went south stopping at each gold camp. Now and then he would meet one of the Georgia men he had staked and the supply of gold he was carrying grew heavier. He wore two pistols, although, he had not yet had to use one of them, and he kept a knife in his right boot.

He had seen enough in San Francisco and heard enough to know that the inconvenience of going around with an arsenal that would have seemed ridiculous back home could forestall trouble before it started out here in the gold fields.

Now, there were only four men left for him to find. Two, he had heard were deep in the Sierras, no one knew just where, the third had left Grass Valley heading for San Francisco as recently as the week before and the fourth was said to be on his way up from the Mother Lode country to the south and would probably reach Sacramento soon and go on to San Francisco. He already had a substantial amount of gold and he longed to go home.

He would come back in a year or two and if Desiree liked it as much as he did, they could sell the store in Dahlonega and start a new establishment in San Francisco where few would bother to look at them and judge their heritage.

Back at Sacramento he ran into Bill Smith, one of the Lumpkin County men who had already heard he was in California. From a hefty sack of gold Bill withdrew the amount he owed Jim. Jim was amazed at the quality of the gold and how well the Georgian had done for himself and he asked him what he planned to do with such a sum.

"I'm goin' to get me a business in San Francisco where I don't never have to bend over a pan or rocker again or sleep on the cold ground and git arthritis. I'm gonna let the miners do the diggin' and spend the gold dust with me," said Bill Smith chuckling.

When he arrived in San Francisco the following afternoon, just to be safe he banked almost all of his gold leaving only enough for the trip home. He took the receipt and made two copies of it—mailing one to Desiree and the other one he kept for himself putting it in the envelope with the lock of Desiree's hair. He held the beautiful, red-gold lock for a moment between his fingers and stroked it before he closed the envelope.

Jim considered spending the night at the El Dorado but decided it was too noisy and went on to the Niantic Hotel. After he cleaned up, he set out for the Chinese section seeking one of the restaurants serving chop suey, the new dish the miners were raving about. Later he strolled back to the square to the crowded El Dorado gambling hall. There was a raucous, joyful whoop and before he knew what was happening he was clutched in an enthusiastic bear hug.

"Jim! I'm glad to see you!" boomed the voice of his old friend, Jake Clay.

"I just got in from the diggin's yesterday and Jeremy told me you were here in California. Of course, Jennie had written you were on your way but that could take months."

Jim found some of the Georgia miners in the El Dorado Bar.
Harper's New Monthly Magazine, 1858

Jim was as glad to see him. Jake had paid his own way West and was eager to tell the story of how he had finally struck pay dirt.

"Us Georgians just know how to mine for gold," he said winking, pleased at Jim's surprise over the amount he showed him. He was replacing the gold pouch in his antelope pocket when they heard a shot ring out followed quickly by two more.

Both men dropped to the floor.

"Where in blazes did that come from?" Jake cried out in the midst of the hullabaloo of voices. There were shouts and crashes of chairs and tables overturning as men hurried to get out.

Jim felt a burning sensation in his chest and when he looked down crimson was seeping from beneath his shirt and spreading across the left side . . . it couldn't be possible. The hard, dangerous journey to get here, the months of traveling from one gold camp to another and now as he was ready to go home someone had shot him. He thought of Desiree's warm beauty and how greatly he loved her. When he looked up at the shining brass lamp hanging above him, there was her face and the baby's reflected in it and then their images began to blur.

Somehow he knew he would never see his wife and child again. It hurt . . . oh, how the knowledge hurt . . . far worse than the pain of the wound in his chest. A terrible sadness and longing enveloped him overshadowing the pain.

Jim was dimly aware that someone was putting something under his head. He saw Jake's face bent over his filled with rage and grief and the faces of the strangers swam around him. Then it no longer seemed he was lying on the floor of the El Dorado Hotel in San Francisco . . . he was back in Dahlonega . . . he was home.

The first letters Desiree received came from San Francisco and were written in June of 1850. They were full of the excitement of this teeming settlement of 25,000 people living in conditions more primitive than Jim had ever imagined. Through the fall and winter letters arrived from one gold camp after another, letters filled with the beauty of the country.

Jim wrote often and she began to enjoy his descriptions and share his enthusiasm. California had just been given statehood and more people were arriving daily. There were thousands of acres of beautiful land and Jim could buy property with no questions asked. He wrote, "I feel that the chains I have worn for a lifetime have dropped from me" and "even if most of these people knew I had mixed blood, it would not interest them."

"My dear, lovely wife, you must see this land and the beauty of the Pacific coast, for I want you to think about our making a fresh start here. Does the idea of traveling all the way across the country frighten you, Desireé? When I can tell you more about it, I don't think you will be frightened . . . you will be excited."

One morning in late fall, Desiree Boisclair went to the post office as was her daily habit.

"There's a letter her for you , Desiree," said Postmaster Gillian.

"From Jim?" she inquired eagerly.

"The writing's familiar but it's not Jim's. Looks more like Jake Clay's," he said holding it up close and peering at the address.

And he was right, the letter was from Jake. He thought she might already have heard the news but he was writing her anyway in the event word had not yet reached Dahlonega. Then the paper began to tremble in her hand almost uncontrollably and she read on with difficulty for as her eyes filled each word was tossing up and down like a small boat in a storm at sea.

"Desiree, I sure hate having to write you this but your Jim is dead. Two days ago he was shot to death at the El Dorado here in San Francisco. He had been to the gold camps where most everyone had paid up, and finally come back to Frisco to collect the last of the money due him and head home.

The hardest thing for me to tell you is that he was murdered by one of our miners, and I damned sure know who did it. There ain't much justice out here yet . . . even less than in the old days in Auraria but don't you worry . . . there's too many of us Georgians out here to let a murderin' skunk live very long. We thought a heap 'a Jim and we're not about to wait around for the law—California style.

Your friend,
Jake Clay

P.S. Desiree, this envelope with the receipt for the gold and the piece of your hair was in Jim's breast pocket. I got most 'a the blood off'n it . . . I'm mighty sorry."

12.
Old Miss Mollie's Back

She stood at the long counter fingering bolts of colorful calico and the sales clerk waited, watching her nervously.

The old woman's homespun dress was ancient. Sleeves wide as buzzard wings flapped about her elbows, seams puckered where they had been resewn many times and the large deep pockets in the front of her skirt sagged.

"Don't know which a these purty patterns I like best," she said, stroking a bolt of bright blue calico admiringly. The pattern on it was pink rosebuds. The clerk cringed for there was dirt in the creases of the roughened hand that caressed the fresh, clean material and the nails were jagged and split.

It was a hot August day in 1834 and so still that not a sycamore leaf nor pine tree needle stirred on either side of the dirt road that was Auraria's main street. The sign in the window of S. T. Rowland's general store said "Cash or Gold." This poor old crittur' hasn't much of either went through the mind of Mr. Rowland's clerk, John Ragan, but he tried his best to be patient with her.

"Mmn, mmn. Just look at them fine hankercheeves," she exclaimed, picking up first a satinett handkerchief and then a silk one. A small gasp of distress escaped Ragan's lips as the hands fresh from the red Georgia clay fondled a fine silken square from London. She raised the silk handkerchief and touched it lightly to her weathered cheek. Poor Ragan turned away unable to restrain a shudder.

"My. Ain't it soft! Puts me in mind of a dress I once had when I was a girl. T'was the only time I felt I was beautiful."

For a moment Ragan felt a stirring of sympathy as he looked at the bushy white eyebrows and weathered features.

"I think I'll take this hankercheeve. How much air it?" she said, raising her eyes to his, and he gave her the price thinking that would be the end of it. To his surprise she reached into one of her sagging pockets, pulled out a scale and then a small chamois pouch.

Thrusting a thumb and forefinger deep inside it she extracted some gold dust and he weighed it. He was about to reach for it to turn it into the metal box in which he kept the gold dust.

"No, ye don't!" she exclaimed. "That's a mite over," and she retrieved a few flecks of her gold.

"I'm sorry Miss . . ." "Just call me, Miss Mollie," said the old lady with faded blue eyes and gray hair streaked with chestnut. She gave him a faint snaggle-toothed smile, stuffed the gold pouch and paper sack into her pocket, and was gone. This was the first time he had seen her but it was not to be the last.

Most often, he would look over under one of the hanging brass whale oil lamps that cast their golden circles in the darker recesses of the store to see her buying hoop cheese, dried beans, cornmeal, or fatback. But sometimes she would stop in the dry goods and her rough, chapped hands would finger the Turkey Red prints, ginghams, and bombazettes. He actually came to like her.

"I ain't never had no dress that nice in my whole life and it sure would make me happy to have somethin' like that someday, even if it were just to be laid out in," she said with a wry grin. He wondered why she cared, for she didn't seem to pay much attention to clothes and always wore the same faded dress. Sometimes she would talk about one of the mines.

"Have you heard what the gold yield is at Battle Branch Mine?"

"No m'am. What is it?"

"Why, they're gettin' a thousand dollars a bushel, Mister Ragan, that's what."

Once he asked her how she knew so much about mining and she replied, "I don't. Before he died, my old man talked about the mines now an agin and I guess, I just larned it from him."

"He worked at one of the mines, did he?'

"Not after he got his legs hurt in the cave-in at the Calhoun. But after he come home for good, he taught me where to go and how to pan to find a bit a color."

"Your claim near the Calhoun?" She smiled. "You ask a lot of questions but you're a good man, Ragan. Yes, it's not far from old John C.'s diggin's."

One morning after Miss Mollie had left, Mr. Rowland said, "You know Miss Mollie ain't poor, I thought you'd a sold her some 'a that blue calico by now. The pattern with the rosebuds on it."

"Well, she sure don't look rich."

"Don't you pay no mind to how folks look, John. You'd be surprised how much gold some of 'em has salted away."

"Maybe so but I don't believe Miss Mollie does."

"I've heard her claim is on the same vein as the Calhoun and they say that vein has been yielding a thousand dollars a day!"

"Whoo-ee!" exclaimed Ragan. but despite Rowland's words, he still felt sorry for Miss Mollie in her dress long since faded to an indeterminate shade of brown. She would admire all the pretty fabrics but she never spent a penny on herself.

That very afternoon she came in the store and bought some fat meat and he saw her look toward the fabric. Wisps of gray hair eluding the knot on the back of her head she stood staring up at the shelves and he noticed that her tanned, heavily lined face appeared more tired than usual. The two big pockets on each side of her skirt sagged halfway to her hem as if she had an iron skillet in each of them, and her arms were red and chapped up to the elbows.

At that moment one of the men from Ira Foster's stables strode in calling out loudly "We done lost two horses and a mare. Now I doan' know what went with 'em an I ain't a goin' to say they was stolen but if any of you folks see 'em. They's a reward."

Customers crowded around him to get a description. About seven o'clock Ragan cleared off the counter, straightened the bolts of cloth on the shelves, and was ready to leave. As was his custom, John locked up and left about a quarter past seven.

He did not own a horse himself and was in the habit of walking the four miles to Traveler's Home, his brother William's inn at Leather's Ford on the Chestatee River. Here he had his own modest room, joined the other guests for dinner at one of the two large tavern tables and later savored a nightly glass of port or claret at the bar.

That night his sleep was fitful and he dreamed. He dreamed Miss Mollie was standing at the counter in the store wanting to see that calico and he pulled it off the shelf, put it on the counter and looked up into her staring eyes. Her eyes were looking at him but not seeing a thing and he was horrified for there was blood all over her head. And the dress . . . the dress was bright blue calico covered with pink rosebuds!

The dream waked him and he sat straight up in bed trembling. He had not changed his candle from the night before and it had burned so low he knew it would be out before morning. The last thing he wanted was to be in the dark so he put a fresh candle into the pewter holder on the table beside him before finally dozing off. He slept poorly until daybreak.

It was mid-day and he had just eaten some New York cheese and crackers and one of the big sugar cookies when Mr. Rowland asked him to take some groceries up to his house " 'cause Miz Rowland is ailin' and needs 'em to start cookin' the evening meal." He went out and saddled Rowland's bay mare, which was kept in a small enclosure behind the store, then hoisted a ham from the large box of salted shoulders, selected turnip greens, weighed out meal and field peas from the wooden barrels and bins and, after loading them in the saddlebags Ragan started off. The house was about three miles from the store.

It was early afternoon as he rode along the main road from town. He had almost reached the Rowland place when he saw a figure approaching him in the distance. It appeared to be a woman and he thought he recognized the ample figure of Miss Mollie.

Her withered, sinewy arms were just a-swinging and her booted feet moved at a fast clip sloughing along in the deep mud of the road. Something unusual about her appearance struck him. He couldn't quite decide what it was. Was it what she was wearing? Or was it the strange angle of her head turned so he couldn't see her face?

He was still some distance away when he called out to her. "You need any help, Miss Mollie?" There was no reply nor did she turn her head so he figured either her hearing wasn't so good or she did not recognize him out of the store.

Suddenly she stepped off the wagon road into the woods near a mammoth oak. He was aware that there at the tree a foot trail started that was a short cut to Auraria. He wondered why she was hurrying so and looked back to see her retreating figure disappear behind a tree and then it was gone. He thought about how foolish his dream of the night before had been.

An hour later with the errand completed for his employer, John Ragan was back at the store. The double doors at the rear were open and some freight wagons from Charleston had just pulled up and were being unloaded. There was cheese, herring, rice, pickles, St. Croix sugar, crackers, mackerel, sperm candles, almonds, tobacco, raisins, Spanish cigars, coffee, New Orleans and New England Rum, Holland gin, cognac, peach brandy, Madeira wine and many items they had needed for weeks so he immediately began grouping them as the barrels and crates were being brought in.

There was so much to unload and the wrapped bolts of fabric were last. He would open and shelve them in the morning. Before he left he rearranged his shelves, consolidating the gingham and prints and making room for the new arrivals.

There was shocking news at Traveler's Home that night. About one o'clock that day, travelers passing near the Calhoun mine in their ox cart had discovered the body of an elderly woman. The couple who had a baby and a small child with them had ridden into town and gone to the sheriff's office. The sheriff and "Doc" Rivers rode back with the man about one o'clock and they had returned with the body.

It was Miss Mollie and it was a mighty bad thing. The poor old woman had been struck on the head with her own shovel and fresh blood was all over her head and the ground around her.

The pick she used to work her claim lay beside her. She was probably murdered for whatever ore she had found that day and "Doc" Rivers thought she had not been dead long when the family happened by.

The talk at the inn disturbed John even more than it did his brother or any of the guests, nor did he want to confide the reason for his agitated state.

Ragan knew that he had looked at his watch when he left the store which must have been only a short time after the strangers discovered Miss Mollie. He had probably just missed them on their way to the sheriff's office. But if Miss Mollie was dead how could he have met her on the road?

The next morning as he let himself in the back of the store, the fragrance he actually looked forward to greeted him. His nostrils inhaled the familiar, pungent blend of aromas of fodder, tobacco, mackerel, herring, and freshly ground coffee. He dropped the first bolts from his arms with a thud upon the dark walnut boards and was astonished to see a disorderly stack of fabric on the floor behind the counter.

The bolt on top of the pile, as if someone had been plundering through the fabrics looking for it, was the blue calico with the pink rosebuds and the end of it was a bit ragged. It seemed to have been hurriedly cut off. Although he never measured a bolt to see how much remained after each purchase, he guessed that at least five or six yards had been removed. Yes, a good deal of the calico was gone.

He had locked the store the night before and at that time all the bolts had been in neat stacks upon the shelves.

When a stranger came by the store to see him just before closing time he couldn't imagine what he wanted. Miss Mollie had been a devout Methodist and it was Preacher William Culverhouse from down in Habersham County asking that Ragan be one of the pall bearers at the funeral next day. They were to meet at the undertaking establishment and the next afternoon he found himself there with five other Aurarians. He felt sad and angry, too . . . angry at the fact that they would probably never know who had murdered Miss Mollie.

For some reason the undertaker was in a most jovial mood.

"Thought we might have to bury the old lady in that dress she used to wear every day but when I went by her house, what do you think I found lying on her bed? It was a nice blue dress with little roses on it. She must have just finished it the night before. Now wasn't that something?"

"Look, gentlemen," and he opened the lid of the pine box with a flourish. There lay Miss Mollie, her strong, work-worn face more peaceful and rested than John had ever seen it in life. In fact, there was a very faint smile on her lips. But what made him gasp was her dress. It was bright blue calico with rosebuds.

He knew now why she had looked different when he had seen her on the road the afternoon before. She had not been wearing the faded old dress she always had on when she came in the store. This was a bright and festive garment and now he realized this was the way he had seen her dressed—both in his dream and on the road.

It was the end of the week and Saturday night when he found it. Just before he left the store he was sweeping the dark places back up under the edge of the shelf where the stock of material was kept. Several small pieces of ore rolled out and he put them in his pocket thinking he would take them to the assay office.

"Mr. Ragan, this is very fine ore," he was told. These are small nuggets but good quality. I can give you these gold pieces for them if you'd like to sell 'em."

Ragan stared at the coins in the palm of the assayer. It was about ten times the price of the calico. He would be able to pay the store for the material missing from stock and re-membering the faint smile on Miss Mollie's face, he couldn't help but think that she had meant the balance of the gold for him.

After her death the *Western Herald* wrote that although her claim was rich she hadn't even owned an ox cart and would walk several miles home every afternoon, her pockets weighted heavily with ore.

In the years after her death a quiet moment would some-times occur during a chuck-a-luck game at Miner's Hall or the Cherokee Hotel and a player would shake his head and swear that only last week he had seen Miss Mollie. It was always on the road from the Chestatee River toward Au-raria; and those who watched the figure striding along were mystified to see her disappear.

"I know I saw her," a miner would say "and she was wearing a blue dress . . . it looked to be bright blue calico."

13.
The Discovery of
Gold in Alabama

His name was Ulrich, he was German and he bought some good Alabama land for a vineyard. It reminds us of two other German settlers, a farmer named John Reed in North Carolina forty years before and ten years later, John Sutter, who planned to raise crops in California.

When Dr. Ulrich arrived in 1840 at the port city of Savannah, he mopped his brow from the heat, looked about him at the flat land and swamps and shook his head. He knew he must travel for miles inland to find country that would look like home. Ulrich's plan was to produce commercial wines.

His ox drawn wagon rolled slowly through east Alabama while Ulrich stared about him at the steep slopes rising from the banks of the Hillabee River and thought the countryside of Tallapoosa County was ideal for his purpose. Later this strip of earth fifty miles long rising above the ground around it would be imaginatively named the Devil's Backbone. He purchased 1,200 acres beside a stream for his vineyard and home. After he completed his house only one important thing remained to do—he must secure his plants. Dr. Ulrich made a special trip back to Germany searching the valley of the Rhine for the best varietal grapes to take back to his vineyards.

As soon as the vines were set out he turned his attention to providing a cool cellar for the wines he would produce and began to dig an immense tunnel into the hillside. "Ach!" he exclaimed excitedly one day while he was digging out the wall of the cave; for a blow from his pick had opened a glittering vein of gold!

147

Ulrich was quite familiar with the gold strikes in the Carolinas and Georgia, and unlike Reed and Sutter, he was ready to forget crops and a winery. The grape vines now grew neglected in the fields while Dr. Ulrich spent his days searching the soil of his land and finding good veins of oxidized ore.

A man of intellect and broad knowledge, he was fascinated by his research into the technology of mining and took readily to modernizing the process. He laid wooden tracks and built small ore cars with mules to pull them. A nearby stream provided the power for his stamp mill to crush the ore.

Rather than make a trip to the mint at Dahlonega with his gold, Ulrich melted it into small, one-ounce bars and traded them for supplies and cattle. Neighbors called his mine the "Dutch Bend Mine" for settlers frequently confused German immigrants with Dutch.

Between 1830 and 1840 Alabama mined a large quantity of gold and nuggets were found that were valued as high as $1,200 each. Prospectors burrowed deep into the red clay soil which had once yielded cotton and corn and called their mines frontier names like "Hog Mountain" and "Lost Dutchman." Near "Hog Mountain" was the boomtown of Goldville with its cock fighting pits, race track and 12 barrooms. The town of Eagle Creek ran a close second with its rowdy games and bars for entertainment starved miners.

By day men from the camps and shantytowns washed sand and gravel from placer deposits along the streams using pans, cradles, sluices, and other devices. When gold became more difficult to trap, they used quicksilver to extract the particles. Just as on North Carolina's Yadkin River, a Cleburne County company used a dredge to recover gold from the soil the rivers had deposited along Dynne and Chulafinee Creeks.

Most gold discoveries were made in the triangular gold belt of northeastern Alabama bordering on Georgia. The belt included Randolph, Cleburne, Clay, Chambers, Coosa, and Tallapoosa counties and parts of Chilton and Elmore counties. Gold towns sprang up along the course of the Coosa or Tallapoosa rivers or were near the small streams that flowed from them. Arbacoochee, Pinetucky, Chulafinnee, and Riddle's Mill were all familiar names to the miners, along with the Idaho district, Cragford, Pinckneyville, Hog Mountain, and the Devil's Backbone.

Arbacoochee soon became the largest town in Alabama with more than six hundred miners working in the gold fields. Prospectors surged into the area from Georgia, North Carolina, and Tennessee. There were twenty general stores, five bar rooms, two mining equipment stores, two hotels, a fire department, a race track, and over a hundred permanent homes.

Here saloon keeper, Dave Kramer, was immortalized for the size of his thumb. There was almost no hard money in circulation and the price of a drink was the amount of gold dust he could hold between his enormous right thumb and his forefinger. Miners found themselves paying Dave about a dollar a drink.

At one time it was thought that Arbacoochee which lies between the Georgia line and the Talladega mountains might even become the capital of Alabama, but today, of the six thousand people who lived in shacks and tents in the area, only three families are left. Like many other boomtowns, gold had given birth to the town and the absence of gold brought about its demise.

When news of the California strike arrived in 1849, miners loaded their wagons, hitched up their horses and oxen and headed west deserting the Alabama boomtowns. Only a handful of old or die-hard prospectors remained poking among the hills for the precious metal, growing discouraged and after a time drifting away.

From the first real strike in 1830 to recent years, about 49,500 ounces of gold have been mined and panned in Alabama with about half that amount coming from Tallapoosa County. Other mines yielded gold in Chilton, Clay, Cleburne, Coosa, Elmore, Randolph and Talladega counties, with the last lodes tapped during the depression of the 1930s.

Records of the U.S. mint show that $367,000 worth of gold mined in Alabama was received between 1830 and 1860. But as is always the case, there was a great deal of unrecorded gold that never reached the mint. It was traded for merchandise at the stores and saloons, melted down for jewelry or found its way into more miners' pockets than we will ever know about.

A paper written by Robert A. Russell of Alexander City and read before the Montgomery meeting of the Alabama Historical Society in April of 1956 describes the gold rush days.

> For the ante-bellum Alabama gold miners all was not gay, lusty, romantic and filled with rich adventure, for mining was then an extremely crude, backbreaking, and for the most part discouraging operation. Their only tools were picks, shovels and buckets. Ore and waste were laboriously drawn from the mines with hand winches or hauled out in rough, hand-constructed wheelbarrows. They did have hand drills and black powder for blasting, but dynamite had not been

invented. Any machinery available had to be hauled by wagons over narrow Indian trails or through dense forests often taking days and even weeks.

The last and most southwesterly section of the East Alabama gold rush occurred in Reptoe district in Chilton County near Verbena. Destined to become a leading producer in the state, the Reptoe mine was worked as early as 1835. It was productive for years but oddly enough the source of the gold here has always remained a mystery.

Alabama gold was formed by molten fluids searing their way into walls of granite. As the molten fluids passed through the granite rock, bits of pure gold were trapped in "quartz stringers" and left imbedded in the rock. Known by geologists as the "Wedowee formation," the gold reserve runs from the northeast corner of Elmore County eastward through Tallapoosa, Randolph and eventually into Cleburne counties.

This geological process left tiny deposits of gold strung like beads throughout northeast Alabama. Deposits were too small to form the gold ore found in the western gold rush. Gold is measured as a percentage of the minerals that surround it; in Alabama, it is measured in parts per million rather than parts per thousand as in the western states. This helps explain why so many miners headed west to California and Colorado.

A cranky mule named "Jude" was responsible for one of Alabama's most exciting gold discoveries reported in Cleburne County. Mrs. J. W. Johnson was plowing one September day in 1938 and Jude didn't want to go over gullies, so to humor the mule, she would stop and fill in each gully with rocks. Jude halted before one of them and as Mrs.

Johnson filled it in, she reached for what she thought was a large rock.

When she succeeded in dislodging it, the rock proved to be a stone bowl and under it she discovered a rectangular, stone-lined hole filled with shining nuggets. The nuggets were later judged to be pure gold worth from twenty-five to thirty thousand dollars.

Because of the primitive manner in which the bowl was fashioned, scholars surmise the gold was hidden there by an Indian prospector centuries ago. A prospector who undoubtedly planned to come back but, perhaps, because of a poor memory or sudden death, never returned.

The treasure cache was found just three miles from the old ghost town of Arbacoochee. Today, weeds fringe the lonely red brick building, once the town hall; the rust-dyed, rocky land is still scarred and pitted from the placer mining of a century ago and the spring breeze stirs the pine trees, brushes the face softly and confides stories of the rowdy, colorful past.

Arbacoochee is a quiet place now and will probably remain so, unless someday another "Jude" comes along.

Part II:

Tales of the

Western

Gold Rushes

14.
The Discovery of Gold in California

The first discovery of gold in California in any quantity was made by a Mexican sheepherder named Francisco Lopez and his helper. It occurred quite by accident for they rode out one day in 1842 from Mission San Fernando to find stray horses in the green valley. They were searching for their horses in a canyon and being hungry they opened a saddlebag and brought out some dried beef and tortillas. Spying a clump of onions, Lopez dug them up with his knife to garnish his tortilla, and found the soil on the roots covered with glittering flecks of gold dust. Lopez and his companion galloped back to the ranch and in the excitement that followed hundreds of people descended upon the canyon to search for gold; washing the streams and pitting the hillsides with their digging. They called this place Placerita Canyon and during the next few years eight thousand dollars worth of gold was found here but the excitement soon subsided.

Like the farmers of the southeast who believed their fortune would be made in crops, the rancheros said to each other, "Why work so hard? Cattle will make us rich. What need do we have for gold?" And Placerita Canyon as it was by then called was abandoned. But at least the discovery of Francisco Lopez made it known that the early myths were based upon some truth.

Thousands of acres were still without settlers and the land was owned by Mexico. To the south of the Sacramento River and not far east of San Francisco, a vast ranch belonged to General Mariano Vallejo. He entertained a Swiss-

155

The first gold hunters.
Harper's New Monthly Magazine, 1858

German named John Sutter and asked him if he would like to stay on and help him, but Sutter, who had landed at Yerba Buena (San Francisco) in 1839 had more grandiose ideas. He envisioned owning thousands of acres which he would run as his own personal kingdom so he approached Governor Alvarado and told him of his wish to own land in California. Alvarado asked where he would like to settle and Sutter who had already framed the answer in his mind to this question replied that he would like to settle in the country near the Sacramento.

He offered to build a fort there in order to guard it against enemies of Mexico or hostile Indians.

The governor was surprised but pleased, and he reminded him that if this land was to be deeded to him, he must first become a Mexican citizen to which Sutter readily agreed. And when the brief ceremony was over the governor deeded over to him fifty-five thousand acres.

Sutter had been wanting this land for a long time. Not only was the Sacramento Valley rich farmland but the Sacramento River was good for sailing vessels and it would be easy to ship things down the river to the harbor at San Francisco. He gathered together ten men, three white and seven Kanakas brought from the Hawaiian Islands and sailed up the Sacramento. This was strange country for him and he leaned on the rail staring at the banks wondering what dangers were there . . . Indians, wild animals? He was convinced he would overcome them and in the midst of his vast acreage he would build a town.

For a week he explored until finally he found an open place at the confluence of the American River and Sacramento River that pleased him. The first grass houses built by the Indians were soon replaced with adobe. Cattle were brought from ranchos to graze in the tall, green grass and crops were planted. Then as adobe bricks lay drying in the sun, the walls of a fort slowly began to rise.

He heard that the Russians were leaving California, for although they had enjoyed a lucrative fur trade they had now killed off most of the otters and they had no interest in farming. Sutter made them an offer to buy everything in the fort and although he had no money at the time, he was fortunate—they accepted his promise to pay as soon as he could. Everything was at the Russian fort that he needed to build his own.

There was a boat to carry materials up and down the Sacramento, lumber, iron tools, and even cannon. With all of this, he could build the finest fort in the West and he did. By 1841 it was completed, a cannon was placed at each of the four corners and overhead there waved a faded Swiss flag. Inside were workshops, a bakery, a blacksmith shop, rooms for the soldiers, and a suite of rooms near the entrance for Captain Sutter, as he was now called. It had, indeed, become like a small town and for a while everyone prospered.

Not a man nor a party of settlers came overland from the east that did not hear of the largesse of Captain Sutter.

"Soon's you get down off the mountains, get to Sutter's Fort," travelers were told. "Captain Sutter will tell you what to do. He'll even give you work . . . or food, if you need it." Sutter paid all his workers in tin money that could be used at the fort.

More people came than could possibly be imagined . . . or needed. There were overland travelers, trappers, Mormons, and soldiers who had fought against Mexico during the war who were now searching for land and for work. Obsessed with the idea of being a sort of burgermeister and military commander combined, John Sutter drilled eighty men as soldiers in his center square. On each half hour during the night the guard would strike a bell by the gate crying out, "All's well! All's well," and so it was . . . for a while.

The westward surge of settlers was underway by the mid-1840s and Californians watched in wonder as they arrived. Why were all these Americans coming to California? It appeared that Americans would take the West! Why was this man, Sutter, welcoming them?

After the fur trappers came those seeking land and opportunity. Young John Bidwell may have been the first
white man to cross the Sierras and stand amazed before the
giant redwoods. And when his exhausted party reached the
last ridge and gazed down into a green valley, off in the
distance was that sight so welcome to many settlers—Sutter's Fort. Far less fortunate was the Donner party in 1846. It
was October and after surviving terrible hardships crossing
the desert the formidable wall of the Sierras stood before
them.

"We must hurry before the snows come," Jake Donner
warned, but they were tired and decided to rest a few days.
Stopping was a horrible mistake. The winter snow came
earlier than usual and caught them. Out of the party of
thirty-one, thirteen died of exposure and starvation. At last
word of their plight reached Sutter's fort and help was
immediately dispatched to these people who had been ten
months on the way . . . but for many who had tried to
survive eating bark and the hides of cattle . . . it was too late.
The tragedy at Donner Pass is one of the more gruesome
stories of the westward migration.

The American flag was raised over the Custom House in
Monterey on July 7, 1846, and shortly afterward an officer
appeared on the fort with an American flag. Slowly Sutter
lowered his threadbare Swiss flag. "It's the end of Mexican
rule," he said to his people in the fort, "Salute . . . salute the
American flag." The Americans were soon to hold all of
California.

It was about this time that Sutter hit on the idea that was
to be his downfall—he decided to build a sawmill. As
builder of the mill he chose a good, trustworthy workman
named James Marshall. Marshall had come from New
Jersey and seems to have been the only millwright in Cal-

ifornia. He had a reputation for being more than a little bit odd, but in addition to being a millwright he was a good mechanic. Together they selected a place where the water of the American River was swift although it was almost fifty miles closer to the mountains. The Indians called the place Colloomah . . . later called Coloma which meant "Beautiful Valley." Marshall selected a curve seeing that the millrace could cut across it from above to turn the wheel below. He would build a road from the fort to the sawmill.

"We can get all the lumber we want and build the mill on the South Fork of the American River. There will be all the power we need and the pine trees we saw down there will bring a good price." Sutter was pleased.

"We'll be partners, Marshall. I'll furnish the men and the supplies, you do the rest."

Marshall, seventeen Mormons, and the Wimmer family who were Georgians left for Coloma. Mrs. Wimmer was to cook for the workers.

"Guardian of the Northern Frontier," everyone called Sutter and he was the happiest he had ever been . . . once this land had been a wilderness but now his barns were full and there were ten acres of gardens and fields of grain watered by wells and ditches. There were hundreds of cattle and sheep and he was ready to meet the needs of the new settlers who were passing through. His dreams had come true and he was convinced that the best years lay ahead.

On the morning of January 24, 1848, Marshall waked early and while the men were preparing breakfast, he walked down to the millrace. They had been digging the ditch to give the mill wheel more space to turn and every night he let the stream run through the race to wash out dirt and gravel. That morning he had a surprise for along the tailrace there were shiny flecks in the earth. Could they be gold? He wasn't sure.

Taking a tin plate he washed out some dirt from the tailrace. The yellow grains were so heavy they went straight to the bottom. It must be gold, but who should he tell about it? Was there anyone he could tell? His decision was no. The next morning he found more golden grains and he pounded some of the little pieces on a stone. He saw that they did not break but flattened out as thin as gold does.

When Marshall showed his golden flecks to the men they only laughed at him, but Mrs. Wimmer from Georgia showed more interest. She was washing clothes in her pot and he dropped some of the gold flecks into a little of the lye water. They were unaffected. It had to be gold.

Rain was pouring down outside when Sutter heard the brass bell ring out. "All's well, all's well," and at that moment there came a pounding on the door. Sutter opened it to face his partner, James Marshall, dripping wet and extremely agitated.

"Captain, I've got something to show you. Lock the door." He asked for scales and Sutter went to bring them leaving the door unlocked. Marshall pulled an old rag from his pocket and opened it to reveal a pile of shiny gold flecks and tiny nuggets. One of the men passed through the room and Marshall pulled the cloth over its contents.

"The men laughed at me and said this was fool's gold but it looks like gold to me, Captain. What do you think?" Sutter held a small piece of ore in his hand and stared down at it. They weighed it and then Sutter found a book with other tests . . . each test indicating gold.

After they had made the tests Sutter sat silently staring into the fire. He was thoughtful, perhaps even a little sad.

"Let's go back there tonight," urged Marshall. But Sutter wanted to wait and to consider what to do. Marshall was impatient to be gone and left a short while later convinced it was gold and eager to get back to guard his discovery. After he had left Sutter began to consider the possibilities of what could happen to him . . . and to his fort. Suppose there was a great deal of gold in the mountains all around the mill. It would belong to everyone and everyone would soon be there. Could the secret be kept? He didn't know but he was going to try.

The following day Sutter saddled his horse and rode to Coloma. He looked at the trace and he found more grains of gold. Saying nothing about this, he gathered some friendly Indians together and told them he wanted to use twelve square miles of land around the mill for a period of three years and he offered them shoes and shirts, knives and flour and other items they needed. In return they agreed that he might have the use of the land.

Marshall agreed to Sutter's idea of offering the men more wages to finish the mill quickly meanwhile keeping the discovery of the gold a secret.

Sutter went back to his fort full of uncertainty about his legal rights to the land and he decided to write the new American governor in Monterey. It was important to clarify his sole right to the land. A messenger was sent with a letter requesting the mining rights but the governor did not know what to reply. It was an interim period between the end of the war with Mexico and the actual signing of the treaty so no one knew what the land laws would be; and the governor sent back word that Sutter could not have the land around the sawmill.

Sutter was apprehensive as to what would happen next. And the news of the discovery of gold at Sutter's Mill was soon out. James Marshall said the Mormons were going around spreading the story. Others thought it was the man who saw Marshall and Sutter examining the gold and still others thought it was the messenger to the governor.

Meanwhile, Sutter himself had been unable to keep the secret. He confided in his good friend John Bidwell who had seen something that looked like gold on his own ranch and returned there quickly to investigate his land. Then Sutter wrote to Mariano Vallejo in Sonoma and told him the "secret." As if that was not enough Mrs. Wimmer wrote home to her family in Georgia telling them that gold had been discovered at Sutter's Creek. A ripple of excitement spread among the experienced miners at Dahlonega for the surface gold there was gone and vein mining expensive.

In fact, she had been panning some herself and when a peddler came up to Coloma with some merchandise she brought out a little bag of gold dust and purchased calico and other personal articles.

The peddler pulled out his bag of gold dust and threw it on the bar counter in Sam Brannan's store to buy himself a glass of ale. When the Mormon, Sam Brannan saw it, he began to make plans. Not only would he sell supplies in his store for mining but he would find gold himself.

Brannan went to San Francisco where he owned the newspaper, the *California Star*, and he inserted a story that a gold mine had been found on the south fork of the American River. The paper in which he placed the story was a special edition describing the wonders of California and it was being mailed back East.

Then he went to Coloma and bought enough gold dust and gold flakes to fill a small bottle. Returning to San Francisco he hurried up to Portsmouth Square where men were standing around talking. Taking advantage of an au-

Buckets of gravel are put into a cradle and rocked so that the gold will settle.
Harper's New Monthly Magazine, 1857

dience and holding the bottle of gold high over his head Brannan stood in the center of the square shouting, "Gold! Gold! Gold has been found on the American River." Men gathered around him to look at it and soon a crowd was listening to his story. Within a few days it was all San Franciscans talked about.

Back at Coloma the sawmill had been finished and the first lumber sent down the Sacramento River to Sutter's Fort but each day there was less time spent cutting logs for the mill to saw into boards and more time spent hunting gold. And it was everywhere. The Mormons were panning, too, and the mill lay idle and forgotten. Even Sutter's colorful Mexican vaqueros had ridden off to the diggings.

In San Francisco stores had begun to close, houses were left half-built, and signs on office doors said, "Gone to the Gold Fields." Everyone was in a hurry to get to Coloma. The few stores that stayed open were those selling shovels, picks, tents, blankets, warm clothes, and mining supplies and they were being bought at any price. By summer San Francisco, which had been a town of nearly a thousand people, was almost deserted for everyone had gone to the mines.

Excitement spread from one town or rancho to another ... get there before the others do. Great chunks of gold are being found ... a dollar a minute!

The *Californian* newspaper stopped publication with a notice that said their readers had left their businesses and were gone.

At Sutter's Fort all work was abandoned. His crops went unharvested and the ring of the anvil was heard no more in the blacksmith shop. The Fort became a place to stop on the way to the mines and only his supply store was flourishing. Sutter did not like the life of a gold miner himself and the Indians and others he hired to mine for him soon left to prospect on their own.

Now, the entire world was aflame with the news ... gold in California, vast wealth to be easily found there ... a treasure that would make a fortune. And so they came— Americans, Chileans, Chinese, Dutch, English, French, Greeks, and the Scotsman in Monterey who was seen staggering down a street as if ill. When someone asked him whether he had caught swamp fever, he replied "Nay, 'tis not the swamp fever. 'Tis a fellow I saw at the tavern about a half hour ago done this to me. He had a lump of gold as big as me fist. Seeing it, and it not mine ... why, it has given me a case of the colic."

And California swarmed with men who had gold colic.

WHO WENT TO THE WESTERN GOLD RUSH?

Who were the men who left the southeast for the California gold fields? All kinds. They were bank clerks, lawyers, ministers, doctors, store keepers, and sons of the prominent—all victims of gold fever, who placed a "Closed" sign on the door of their office or place of business and left. Then there were the gamblers and thieves who arrived to prey on the rest.

Many of the most venturesome and hardy forty-niners had panned and dug in the rolling countryside of Virginia, the Carolinas, Georgia, Tennessee, and Alabama. These experienced southeastern miners were the ones most likely to find gold.

They were at home with a rifle, could drink from a pool in a rock and strain tadpoles through their mustaches, gather wood for a campfire in barren places, and find a sheltered place where they could sleep on the ground in their blanket. They could stand off hostile Indians, ride a mule for miles without a map, cross foreboding, uninhabited country, brave rugged mountains, deserts, swamps, epidemics and live with the ever present possibility of death. Nor was there any guarantee that if they were finally lucky enough to get there they would find gold. Yet thousands went.

The majority traveled overland by mule, oxen and on foot taking several routes. Others took passage on anything afloat along the eighteen thousand mile route around Cape Horn to San Francisco. While still others tried to save time by heading for the isthmus of Panama and cholera ridden Chagres where they either struggled through the jungle or took a boat on the Chagres River to Panama City. From there they joined others impatiently awaiting passage to San Francisco.

The first census in California was in 1850, when many men from the southeastern states had already arrived. A partial list of southern prospectors in Calaveras County follows:

From Virginia, there was H. Albright, David Alexander, and James Moffet; from North Carolina, William Abbot, Mark Aker, Benjamen W. Morton, David Nixon, Hannah and Al M. Page, Carles Perkins, James W. Pratt, C. M. Shelton, Daniel and Leander Amick, Chessen Batton, Edmond B. Stephens. Of the South Carolinians in Calaveras, there was John R. Myatt, John Osborne, Watt Porter, and John Quigby; Tennesseans in this census were J. G. Aisen, Hugh and J. A. Allison, V. G. Allen, John Rankin and Edward Shackleford. Georgians had come in abundance and among them were Zacary Acosta, E. G. Miller, E. and Quincy Montrose, George W. Parks, Carter Pratt, James Reed, A. C. Ryan, Robert Rutledge, J. W. Samuel, W. Philo Sanders, Thomas Scott, Lewis Shaw, S. P. Stampe, C. P. Stickell, George Stockwell, Albert Strong, George and James Thomas, Thomas Tice, S. Toogood, Hiram Vanpelt, C. S. Walrath, John Z. Andrews, Eldridge B. Barnes and William G. Smith of Lumpkin County.

Most of the Georgians were twenty to thirty years old and many had abandoned the mines in their own state to go to California. Many of the North Carolinians and Virginians were in their thirties and forties and familiar with the early, rich days of the gold rush in the southeast.

The names above came from the census of just one California county in the gold country; but there were southerners prospecting all over the West. Undoubtedly, they were among the most experienced miners in California, and among them were men like Green Russell and John Gregory who were both destined to become famous.

15.
A North Carolinian Shapes California

His letter to President Santa Ana asking for his release from prison went unanswered, but Brigadier General Thomas Green had known it was a gamble. It was his misfortune and one of the ironies of fate that he himself had once captured and held Santa Ana. He and the other Texans had been made prisoners in December of 1842 after the Battle of Mier and marched on foot to the dungeons of that grim Mexican fortress, Castle Perote.

When no response came to his letter the General knew only one course remained—to attempt escape. He might fail but if he did he would die trying.

Most of the captured Texans could speak only the most commonplace Spanish phrases, but Green could converse in the language with fair proficiency. Soon he was able to gain the confidence of one of the prison guards, Miguel, an ambitious fellow who believed the General's offer of money and assistance in starting a new life in Texas.

The first step was to get himself placed in a cell alone. It was not safe to try to take any of the others with him. He must work for their release from Texas. He and Miguel devised a scheme. Miguel claimed Green had cursed him and transferred him to solitary confinement where he was given half rations. Confined now for almost a week, he would have certainly have begun to lose some of his strength had not his confederate smuggled food to him from the guard's mess table. Miguel also brought him "carne" and it was meat he needed if he was to keep up his strength.

On the sixth night of his solitary confinement they were ready to implement their plan. He knew it would be after midnight before Miguel, bearing the clothes of a Mexican and a stilleto, would come back to unlock the door to his cell.

Green was to conceal these clothes, lie down and pretend to be asleep when the next guard on duty made his check. He could not dress before the guard looked in, for he had no sheet with which to cover himself. The lock would be in place but a slight twist would open it—if the check by the guard was merely perfunctory, all was well. But, if he should test the cell door even routinely, it might open.

Then General Green had two choices—either allow his friend to be punished for carelessness or to quickly subdue and gag the guard . . . nor did he rule out the stiletto for if the guard cried out all was lost.

When the guard passed on he was to dress as quickly as he could, use the key he would find in the pocket of the pants to unlock an exit not far from his cell and meet Miguel a short distance away on the road where he would be waiting with two horses.

Green lay on the bunk and the moon shown through the bars. It was after midnight and he fingered the handle of the stilleto in the pocket of his ragged uniform pants. Where was Miguel? Why didn't he come? He heard the sound of soft, stealthy footsteps and his heart began to pound.

The footsteps were faster now and closer. General Green sprang up from the bed of cornshucks on the floor and went over to the bars. Now the footsteps reached his cell and stopped. But it was not a man, it was one of the half-wild dogs that hung about the castle hungry for the poorest sort of scrap. With a curse he frightened the animal off and lay back down.

Where was his friend? He feared the time was approaching for the change of guards and then the presence of Miguel, known to be off duty, would be regarded with suspicion.

"General!" whispered a voice and he saw a dark shadow. It was Miguel hurriedly thrusting the clothing through the bars into his outstretched hands and then he was gone. Green lay back down, the clothes folded beneath the small of his back, and tried to look as if he were asleep. The new guard would be here soon. A cloud had drifted across the moon and the darkness would help conceal him for it was desperately hard to assume the pose of a relaxed, sleeping man when every nerve was taut.

A door clanged and he waited for the sound of the guard's tread. He was the only man in solitary at present. Would the guard inspect more carefully because of this? The fellow was humming some Spanish tune when he came up to the small cell and the general did not stir.

The humming stopped as the man stared in . . . there was a hiccup, the strong odor of tequila and then silence. Was he suspicious of something? Could he reach him and put an arm about his throat before the man cried out? Should he try for a swift stab with the stiletto? Green prayed fervently and lay upon the cornshucks as still as death. Then he heard a step, and another and another. The door clanged shut and the guard was gone.

Within seconds he was pulling on the clothes Miguel had brought him . . . clothes ridiculously small for a man of his height and build but it didn't matter. Where was the key? It was not in the pocket! He turned them inside out in terrible frustration. He was dressed but how would he get out? Then he felt something beneath his bare foot and realized in his haste the key had fallen to the floor. Fifteen minutes later he and Miguel were riding toward the Texas border. They had at least a four or five hour start on any pursuers.

Safely back in Texas, Green returned to the legislature to work for the freedom of the still imprisoned Texans in Mexico, also introducing a bill to make the Rio Grande the boundary line between his adopted state and Mexico.

Miguel stayed on with him and they rode over the land for a town at the mouth of the Brazos River. It was to be called Vellasco and the general laid it out and purchased the acreage along with his partners, Dr. Branch Archer and the Whartons of Tennessee. But before Texas became a state, he returned to his home in North Carolina.

He was on a trip to see a classmate in Boston when he met a beautiful widow whose husband had been a friend of his and the general who had been a widower himself for a decade proposed marriage to her.

"Thomas," said she, "I hope all those dangerous adventures of yours have ceased and that we may spend the balance of our lives peacefully in our Boston and North Carolina homes."

"I can think of nothing better," agreed the General and at the moment he meant it.

In June of 1845 Adeline E. Ellery married Brigadier General Thomas Nelson Green in as impressive a wedding as most Bostonians had ever seen. There were no attendants for both the bride and groom were widowed and in their forties. But Adeline Ellery was a handsome woman and as she had walked down the aisle on her brother's arm in her Parisian peach satin dress embroidered with glittering jet beads a murmur of admiration arose from the guests in the church.

The wedding was followed by a reception at her mansion and as everyone entered the dining room they saw a profusion of peach colored roses. Of course, there was Waterford crystal, English silver candelabra, and a magnificent wedding cake.

Of course, the Bostonians talked. Where was the home of this Thomas Nelson Green who had captured their beautiful Mrs. Ellery? Gossip had it that he was from some crossroads in North Carolina but they could forgive that for he had graduated from West Point and as a Brigadier General had fought beside the Texans in the war against Mexico.

Others said he had also served in the state legislatures of both Florida and Texas; and everyone knew he had been in Boston visiting a former West Point classmate when he and Adeline had met. But the guests were most awed by his daring escape from the dread Mexican prison, Castle Perote, after the Battle of Mier.

The wedding over, Green was eager to return to his North Carolina plantation home, "Esmeralda" on Shocco Creek near Warrenton. His only son, Wharton, was a student at Lovejoy's Military Academy in Raleigh and he had seen little of him for the past several years. It was summer and Wharton would be at the plantation.

The best families at Warrenton did their utmost to entertain Adeline although she could scarcely have been less impressed by what seemed to her a "frontier society." Warrenton was to prove entirely too quiet for the Boston belle. She merely tolerated the months they spent at "Esmeralda," but her brown eyes sparkled and she betrayed an almost girlish animation when they returned to Boston, for here at home she enjoyed the theater, balls, musicals, fine restaurants, and the stimulating life she had always known.

General Green himself chaffed at the slow pace of a small farm community and spent considerable time in Washington City as the capital was then called. His first wife, the daughter of the Honorable Jesse Wharton of Tennessee, had lived only five years; and for an entire decade between her death and his remarriage the General had been a soldier of fortune, living a life full of travel, danger, and adventure.

"More coffee, dear?" There was no answer and Adeline knew the General was so deep in thought he had not even heard her. He had scarcely touched his breakfast. It was 1849 and the couple were visiting in Washington. Although they were almost two weeks into April, the city still looked wintry and the cherry trees were only beginning to come out. They had been married four years and Adeline knew his moods well. A man addicted to action, he had been restless for weeks, she thought. In fact, ever since he had heard of the gold discovery in California.

Their friends, even her brother, could talk of little else and many had already left but the General knew how she felt about his going.

"You are thinking about it again, aren't you, Thomas?"

"About what?" And it was as if his thoughts were returning from a long distance.

"You were thinking about going to California . . . making a fortune digging for gold and all that sort of foolishness."

"And why is it so foolish?"

"A man almost fifty years old making such a dangerous trip?"

"My dear, I'm not fifty. I'm forty-eight and I think I have had ample experience with danger."

"More than enough!" said his wife. "What about savage Indians? And, if you are fortunate enough to escape them, there are cholera epidemics and simply dreadful hardships on the way."

"I have survived Boston winters and Mattilda's efforts to make edible southern biscuits," he said, smiling at the sparks in his wife's eyes. "Adeline, I am more able to survive hardship than many of those who are setting out each day."

"You are not going to be happy until you go out there, are you?"

"Probably not, Adeline."

An hour later as he sat at the mahogany secretary in the parlor writing, Adeline came up beside him and looked down at the letter.

> "Honorable William Ballard Preston
> Secretary of the Navy   April 11, 1849
>   Sir:
>   Having tried in vain to get passage to California via Panama, I find that my only prospect of accomplishing my journey readily is to go through the city of Vera Cruz . . ."

"Thomas! You have tried to get a boat passage to California and never told me!"

"My dear, I would have told you the moment I obtained it." The General covered her hand with his and looked sheepish. Then he put down the pen and rising began to pace up and down the room.

"All right. You shall go. But don't expect me to set out with you in any covered wagon!" He hugged her to him and tried to sooth her.

"Of course, I don't. You would miss your friends and all the parties. I won't be out there long—just a few months."

Denied the assistance he requested from the Secretary of the Navy, General Green decided to take the risk of going through Mexico anyway but he mentioned little of this to his wife. By the time his arrangements were made, Adeline had resigned herself to his absence and was even encouraging him in his plans to acquire mining interests which he had given the ambitious name of "New Horizons Company." A friend of his from his military days, Colonel John McLemore of Tennessee, hoped to join the General the following October and wrote him that he had heard three companies were forming—one under military organization to work the placers, the second was a Scotch company and a third was an American company.

"I hope you may manage to get an interest in some of these and make a fortune before you get to San Francisco," wrote the optimistic Colonel McLemore.

General Green wouldn't have missed the California gold rush for anything! Born in Warren County, North Carolina in 1801 he was so familiar with gold mining in his home state that he invented and patented an improved gold rocker. He would know what to do when he got there. On his way West he saw signs in store windows saying, "Get your shovel here, none in California, bags and belts to hold your gold, take plenty of food, if you don't you will starve," but he paid no attention.

Green did not plan to dig for gold. There were many men quld stake to do that ... he had brought money to buy land and despite cholera, bandits, Mexicans, and other hazards he reached San Francisco safely.

Despite all he had heard, the city was more primitive than he had expected ... tents, shacks, log cabins, and muddy streets crowded with red-shirted miners. His first step was to visit the mayor and offer his services. There was a desperate need for law and order in the chaotic settlement and the mayor was glad to enlist the assistance of a cou-

Major General Thomas Green of the California Militia traveling north to suppress Indian disturbances.
Harper's New Monthly Magazine, 1858

rageous general who spoke both Spanish and English and understood gold rushes.

Green was first made Major-General of the California Militia and sent to suppress Indian disturbances which he handled with dispatch. Returning to the San Francisco area many other ventures attracted his interest.

When California became a state on September 6, 1850, General Green was proposed as a candidate for the first legislature, ran and was elected state senator. A graduate of the University of North Carolina at Chapel Hill, one of his most important pieces of legislation was to introduce and pass the bill for the establishment of California's first state university. He was also among the earliest advocates of a railroad to the Pacific.

He acquired considerable land holdings, helped lay out the towns of Oro and Valejo, and appointed a prospector from Illinois, James M. Burr, as first Port Commissioner of Valejo. In a short time, this North Carolinian had become an influential, respected citizen.

But California was not to be his permanent home for no entreaties were able to convince Adeline to live such a distance from her beloved Boston. After serving his term, General Green became more and more homesick for her and his son, Wharton, and on the 15th of May, 1852, he sailed out of San Francisco on the steamer, *Winfield Scott* . . . North Carolina bound.

General Thomas Nelson Green was probably North Carolina's most colorful and outstanding contribution to the early days of the California gold rush.

16.
Off to the Gold Rush

Adventures of James Burr, related in letters to his wife Caroline in Illinois. General Thomas Green of Warrenton, North Carolina, appoints Burr first Port Commissioner of Vallejo & Benicia, California.

December 29, 1850
New York

Dear Caroline,

I promised to write again after leaving New York. I shall now attempt to do it in my own simple way. You must know that we were all supposed to go to California together. That is our company which consists of Colonel McLemore [a Tennessean], myself, Henry Burr, and Henry May. Mr. May and myself were ready but the rest were not; consequently we must wait for the next steamer which will be on the 11th of January. At that time we expect to sail.

You no doubt think I'm enjoying myself here. It is true, I am in some respects. At least I aim to do so to kill time but the truth is I feel very much unsettled. I either want to go or return where I can enjoy myself with you and the children. In regards to the children, how did they spend Christmas? Did they hang up their stockings? Tell them, I should like to have been there to fill their stockings.

I have been looking for a word from you for some time. I feel quite disappointed at not hearing a word since I left. You know, you may possibly have time to write me in answer to this. At any rate you can write. If I do not get it,

179

sister Addeline, will forward it to me. We have an abundance of snow and if you have as much in Como I hope you will make Rubin keep plenty of wood. Will see that everything is paid up before leaving, to the satisfaction of yourself and my creditors.

Tell the children to be good and go to school.

From your loving husband,

J. M. Burr

January 10, 1851
New York

Dear Caroline,

I now sit down to write you for the last time from this place as we leave tomorrow morning for California. Colonel McLemore and Henry Burr will not go in this steamer but will follow soon. Now, my own dear wife, I have been here a good while and I regret exceedingly that I could not get one word from you or from Como, Illinois before leaving.

As regards my affairs and to make you happy, I have just placed in my sister Addeline's hands one hundred and fifty dollars to be paid into hands of the company and from which you will be able to draw from them. The balance, a hundred and fifty more, will also be coming shortly. I am sure she will be glad to comply with all my requests as she has always done.

Now for a few words of consolation. As it is twelve o'clock at night and every soul is in bed and I have my trunk to pack up yet, my dear Caroline, rest assured that my whole aim is for your comfort and the dear children. I want you to keep up your good spirits and think it all for the best that I am about to take such a journey and may I have your good prayers. Kiss the children often for me and remind them of their old Papa and if it is God's pleasure for me to prosper, they shall one day all be made happy.

Write me as soon as you get this and direct your letters to me care of General T. J. Green, San Jose, California.

January 28th, 1851

Dear Wife,

On the morning of the 22nd I arrived in Chagres having very rough water as we tried to land. From here we took a small steamer and made our way up the river. We tied up and slept, or tried to, in the boat for they charge fifty cents for the privilege of sleeping under a cover on the ground. A dollar for what they call a meal.

Thursday the 23rd was employed getting up the Chagres River the best way we could. Saw nothing remarkable but a fine river. Slept upon a sand beach. Friday the 24th we started at daylight, saw nothing but one man laying drowned and the buzzards eating him. Arrived at Corgana about noon and I saw a small village built up on poles. Indians, Negroes, Spaniards, Yankees and all countrymen. This night, Friday the 24th, we loaded up our mules and launched out for the isthmus. Travelled all this day and laid upon the ground at night with about seventy-five Californians returning and about twenty-five of us which made about a hundred of us strewn all over the ground to sleep.

Saturday the 25th, we got our mules loaded up and started about seven o'clock in the morning without supper or breakfast not feeling disposed to pay one dollar for such as we get over in Panama. About noon went to the mansion house at two dollars per day. Sunday the 26th, this morning, quite an excitement prevailed.

"We loaded up our mules and launched out for the isthmus." - J. M. Burr.
Harper's New Monthly Magazine, 1858

The circumstances are these. Two months ago a man by
the name of Hans, an American, was confined in prison for
killing his brother-in-law. Last night he managed to get a
bottle of brandy with poison. He then poison treated the
drinking water gourd. Three officers were found dead.
They held a post mortem examination and went to do the
operation, the most horrible sight I ever saw.

One of them had his scalp taken off to examine his brain
with the prisoner present. He is to be shot in a few days
together with two more men that robbed the special train.
We shall probably witness the scene . . . I have been trying
today to get on the ship without buying a full passage. I have

some encouragement to go on the steamboat Columbia as its butcher. If I get the job, I get my passage free and five dollars. That is about equal to one hundred fifty five dollars saved, passage being one hundred and fifty dollars.

Our friend, Colonel John C. McLemore, gave me a letter to a Mr. Turner at Chagres. I could find no such person. After arriving in Panama made inquiries and finally found he had been engaged as a bank clerk there in the firm of Corwin & Company, instead of being a forwarding agent, and that he had left for San Francisco about a month ago.

I have just engaged to go on the steamer Columbia as butcher. My pay is $5. I find it necessary to begin to make money whenever an opportunity affords.

Your loving husband,
J. M. Burr

February 13, 1851
Iumaca Plains

Dear wife,

It is with great difficulty that I write you this morning as the state of my affairs are such as not to mention. To give you an idea of my situation. I have at this present time due me in this town about $700 from the bank and in debts and merchandise. The removal of the capitol of California to Sacramento which took place late last night broke everyone flat. I was present in the hall at the time it was decreed.

I am going to the mines to try my luck there. If I don't succeed, you may expect me home as soon as spring opens. You need not expect any money which I promised to send you soon. If I had got what was due me here I had intended to send you $500 in a few days but now I cannot say positively if I ever can recover my debts. If I recover my debts all will be right again. If not I shall have to dig it first and that you know is mighty uncertain, therefore, you must keep up good courage and I trust all will be right yet. I hope you will not neglect to write me every mail for you have no idea the anxiety I have to hear from you as I have not heard one word since I left.

Give my best love to all. Kiss all the children for me a dozen times over and believe me yours forever.

James M. Burr

P.S. I want you to direct your letters to me at Sacramento City care of Mrs. Merrill and she will forward them to whatever part of the gold country I am in.

February 26, 1851
San Jose

Dear Caroline,

I only arrived here yesterday in San Francisco, about noon, after a hazardous and tedious passage of 26 days up the California coast what with losing our rudder, boat caught on fire several times, getting out of Chagres covered with bugs, a great many ticks, and many men dead (we hove the last poor fellows overboard last Sunday). I have enjoyed very good health myself as yet.

Leaving San Francisco this morning we arrived in San Jose at three. Found General Green in good health. As yet I can give you no idea of what I shall do. . . .

Your loving husband

Note: Although he did not encounter Turner, by great good fortune he did meet his friend Colonel John C. McLemore of Tennessee who gave him a letter of introduction to Green. McLemore had arrived in California in the fall of 1849 to join General Thomas J. Green of Warrenton, North Carolina. Although he arrived only a little more than a year before, General Green quickly became a man of influence and a member of the senate of the first California legislature. Due to McLemore's glowing recommendations he is ready to appoint the by now penniless Burr from Illinois to a prestigious position but one which had few duties at the time.

March 11, 1851

> Office of the Secretary of State
> San Jose

James M. Burr, Esquire
Sir:

I have the honor to transmit herewith your commission as one of the Port Wardens of Benicia and Vallejo. Before entering on the duties of your office you will take the oath of office, see the Constitution, a copy of which should be endorsed on the back of your commission and transmit the original to be filed in this office.

> Very respectfully,
> Your servant, W. Dan Oorhuis

> [Excerpt]

Dear Caroline,

Mr. May and myself walked down to Vallejo the other day and at the place found nothing but a few tents. If they don't set me at work soon, I shall go to the mines . . . I see hundreds from the mines every day. Some tell good stories and some poor ones. A person knows no more about California here than you do at home.

I have been appointed Port Warden and have sworn to faithfully discharge the duties of Port Warden for the ports of Benitia and Vallejo. What I expect to do is this—to lay out a plan and afterwards to put up a house, if I can make some money on lumber. Mr. May and myself are well which I hope may continue for this place is not fit for a sick person. I find people have to work as hard here as at home. Here we see all sorts of people and some pretty hard cases.

The gambling houses at San Francisco are quite a curiosity—a large hall with a band, music, some dozen tables filled with gold and silver, a great many ladies engaged in gambling at the tables.

> April 29, 1851
> Vallejo

Dear Wife,

I have just a few minutes to write owing to the difficulty in sending. I am in Vallejo and am doing nothing at present as large bodies move slowly. I expect soon to do something. I am here at Vallejo at work fixing up the principal hotel. Case Wilson is my bedfellow. I am waiting for General Green to come up here from San Jose. You may not expect much news from me for the present for this place is new and it is five miles up to Benicia. Oh, how I miss you and the children. I have not yet had one letter from you.

> May 14, 1851
> Vallejo

Dear Caroline,

I hope in the future you can be more punctual in your writing. I don't want to scold you, but I do want to know how you and the children are. Mr. May gets letters every mail and I have not had but one since my arrival in California.

I have not seen General Green for a month but he is expected here tomorrow and the great sale of lots comes off on the 19th of our great city of Vallejo. Mr. May is cutting hay here at $5.00 an acre. Carpenters are getting $8 and $10. Board is $10 to $12 dollars per week. I cannot say much for California as I have not seen much of it as yet but the climate is good.

June 25, 1851
Vallejo [Excerpt]

Dear Caroline,

It is June 25th and I am up in the mountains. I am happy to say I received three letters from you. Two weeks ago General Green sent up from San Francisco, scythes, rakes and pitch forks saying the hay business was the best thing we could go into. Hay was then selling in San Francisco for $80 per ton and would probably be $100.

Mr. May, Captain Joaquin and myself, took our tent and went out in the mountain valleys to cut oats. We pitched our tent in the American Canyon about five miles from the city of Vallejo where we now are and shall probably be about a week.

We are in a valley surrounded by mountains covered with herds of horses, wild cattle, coyotes and wolves. We have a tent, sleep on the ground, rather a solitary life especially when some go into town for provisions which is bread and meat. We have cut about 30 tons, the three of us in two weeks. We have it yet to stack and send to the market.

I sent you by last mail some papers giving an account of the great fire at San Francisco. While at Vallejo I saw a great smoke down the bay and remarked that San Francisco was burnt up again and the news has just come that it has. It is thought it was set afire about a week ago. They caught Sidney Cases, as they termed them, stealing an iron safe and called a number of citizens together and hung the fellows on the same day in the plaza on the old arcade building.

Yesterday they caught a gang of them. They shot one, hove one in the flames and burnt him up, tomorrow they hang twelve more by order of Judge Lynch. This is a great country, it is no place for an honest person.

Feb. 10th/52
Kelsey's Dry Diggings

Dear Caroline,

I have but a few minutes to write in as the mail leaves to night. Therefore can say but little more than I am well. We are living up in the mountains in a log cabin. Our fare is rough—beans three times a day. We have been up to our knees in mud for three weeks digging away like fury. Have got some dirt stored up. But owing to the scarcity of water have not washed any yet. I am unable to say when I shall come home but am in hopes of striking upon something soon which will enable me to come soon. I have to walk six miles tonight to get home as Porter and myself have been prospecting and strayed down to Coloma at Sutter's old mill.

My best respects to all the neighbors, the little girls and yourself.

Kelsey's Dry Diggings Feb 25th

Dear Caroline,

It is with pleasure that I am permitted to write you again in good health but not in good spirits. . . . I have been up here in the mountains five weeks. Porter and myself live in a log cabin and have to travel two miles for our grub (food) which we run in debt for and this being Sunday and our wash day we have just got through with that job. The next was our dinner of bread, beans and cofffee.

We have been looking for letters for the last two weeks but to no effect. I was in hopes of hearing from you before I wrote again. Have sent over to Coloma, 7 miles, the nearest post office as we have 2 mails that come in from the States and have got no letters from either. We are digging away in hopes of striking upon something.

We have no water to wash the dirt. Although, it's the rainy season we have no rain. I think I shall stay about here a short time longer and if nothing turns up better than what we have found I shall leave for some other mines and give it a fair trial before leaving. And, if I don't succeed I shall try to work my way home, for it's too discouraging.

[Excerpt April 25, 1852]

We are digging away in hopes of striking something. . . . I want to see you bad enough and the little girls. (In my dreams I see little Addeline's golden curls) but cannot stand the idea of coming home without money. Now I am here I want to give it a fair trial.

[Excerpt May 12, 1852]

I notice what you said in your letter about having to go into the Dairy Business and how bad you need money. I wish it was in my power to send you some, but I have to dig it—yet I still live in hopes of striking upon something any day. I let Colonel McLemore have two hundred dollars which I presumed he would of said something about before leaving for the States. He left without repaying it.

[Excerpt November 12, 1852]

We are hard at work heaving up dirt and preparing to wash it when the rains come. We hear cholera is bad in Sacramento. I am in hopes of coming home in flying colors by next April. I was over to Placerville Sunday in hopes of seeing some one from home but could not. Lots of families came in across the plains. I pitied them. . . .

I want to come home as bad as you want me to come but hate to come without money for I don't want to be laughed at. I see by your letters you are enjoying yourself which I am much pleased to hear. I send you by this mail another draft of 50 dollars being three. I have sent you, my pretty face, a handsome breast pin, three bank drafts of 50 each and want you to write me whether you receive them or not.

March 13, 1853

My prospects for doing well depend upon the rains and length of time I stay here. My intention is to leave here the first of April but maybe not until May."

Note: James Burr chose the lure of the gold fields rather than staying on in his position in Vallejo where he might well have become one of its prominent founding citizens. This was the last letter available from Burr to his wife, Caroline. He returned to Illinois the summer of 1853.

Did he hit "pay dirt" or did wealth elude him? Research discloses that today, Como has virtually disappeared from the map giving way to the town of Sterling, Illinois. But the Burr family was a prominent one in the area. James M. Burr was one of seven children of a ship captain, James Madison

Burr. According to biographical data from Sterling, James M. Burr, Jr. returned to Como following "three successful years in the gold fields."

After the amateur prospector's hazardous trip to California and all the digging and heaving of dirt in Kelsey's Dry Gulch, it would be sad to discover that his worst fears had been realized and that he had come home empty-handed to be derided in Como! Happily, James Burr was able to purchase extensive holdings of farm land with the gold he brought back from California.

Several years later his daughter whom he called in one of his letters, "Addeline with her golden curls," married Wharton J. Green, son of General Thomas J. Green of Warrenton, North Carolina, whom Burr had met in California.

Shortly after James and Caroline Burr celebrated their fiftieth wedding anniversary in Como in 1890, James Burr died. His widow, Caroline, left Illinois to live the rest of her life in North Carolina with Colonel and Mrs. Wharton Green.

And this is how the California gold rush brought two prominent families from Illinois and North Carolina together.

17.
Green Russell:
A Man Without Fear

There were days in his life the tall, rawboned farm boy from Auraria, Georgia, would always remember and this would be one of them. Rising on an icy winter morning in 1833 and still shivering as he went out to feed the livestock, William Green Russell was startled by the dazzling brightness of everything around him. He looked up to see the darkness surfeited with blazing stars that soared, careened across the sky and plumeted to earth. Was the world coming to an end as he had often heard preachers predict? Had doomsday arrived?

As his father came out of the house Green started to run toward him, then, noticing his complete absence of fear, he stopped. For James Russell stood gazing up at the sky his face filled with wonder. The boy would never forget his father's composed manner and his dismissing the shooting stars as a sign of judgment. Others were not so calm and in Auraria the most hardened gold miners, never before known to pray, were on their knees repenting of their sins. It was November 13, 1833, the morning "stars fell on Georgia."

And, if not a sign of the supernatural, it was still very much in keeping with the star-crossed life Green Russell was to lead.

Born in 1820, one of six children of this pioneer family who had moved from Pennsylvania to the north Georgia foothills; Green was nine years old when gold was discovered. For a while life remained unchanged. Like other boys in a rural area, he would wake to see the Blue Ridge in the distance, spend his days plowing and hoeing the fields with his father and daydream after dusk when his labors were over.

The beautiful, rolling countryside belonged to the Cherokee Nation and since his friends were more often Indian than white he would head for one of the Cherokee farms and go off with the youths to hunt or trap small game. They taught him to track animals, how to anticipate danger, what roots and berries could be safely eaten, and how to survive in the wilderness—knowledge that would someday be invaluable.

By the time Green began playing with his Cherokee friends, many of their parents could read and write. "Talking leaves," pieces of paper with marks upon them, were no longer looked upon as magic. Sequoyah, the man the superstitious Indians first suspected of being a witch doctor had taught them his invention, the Cherokee alphabet of eighty-two characters. The Cherokee national council made Sequoyah's alphabet official and sent him around the nation to teach everyone to read and write. Within six months most had learned the alphabet and the Cherokees were now the first Indian tribe to have its own written language.

Word of the gold discoveries spread with the speed of a forest fire and hundreds of gold lusting men flowed into Auraria and Dahlonega. Green watched them wonderingly as they strode down the main street of Auraria and overnight he saw the town change. Men drunk whiskey freely in the numerous taverns and there were chuck-a-luck gambling games everywhere. Stakes were high and they played with a hotheaded recklessness that led to more than one brawl.

In greedy haste, the state held a mammoth lottery dividing its mineral lands into forty-acre lots and apportioning them to lucky ticket holders. Meanwhile a motley crew of fortune seekers overran the Indian lands squabbling over claims and every day more wild-eyed men with spades, pans, and rocker cradles thronged into north Georgia to dig in the red clay hills and wash sand and gravel beside the streams. They were rough fellows who protected their diggings with guns. Green was both fascinated and repelled by what he saw.

Gold attracted the famous and the infamous and at the village of Auraria, in the wilds of northern Georgia, men sat around the table at Ma Paschal's tavern and talked of rich veins, of mother lodes and fortunes made and lost—men like John C. Calhoun, Thomas Jefferson Rusk who would become a prominent U.S. senator and author, and William Gilmore Simms.

Since gold had been discovered near Dahlonega and in the adjoining county nothing had been the same for the Cherokees. The gold was in surface or "placer" deposits, rich and easily worked and it invited intrusion on their land. While Chief John Ross was away in Washington, a handful of Indians met and signed an illegal treaty agreeing to give away all their lands in Georgia and Alabama and move the people west of the Missippippi. This spelled tragedy for the Cherokees. Gold seekers and renegades spilled over into the Cherokee Nation and they were not always peaceful.

Green helped his father work a small claim but mining was hard work and James Russell's health began to fail. After his death in 1835 William Green became head of the household, assuming a patriarchal position that he would hold for the rest of his life.

John C. Calhoun's mine was near Auraria and Green's mother admired the Senator. On Calhoun's visits he stayed at Grandma Paschal's place and his stern ways won the strong-willed old lady's good word in the community. Calhoun offered Green a job at his mine, one of the richest in Auraria, and his two brothers, Levi and Oliver soon joined him. Green worked side by side with Calhoun's slaves, loners who were down on their luck, former store clerks, merchants, bankers, doctors, lawyers, and men from every way of life imaginable. He learned quickly from the more experienced miners and their stories stimulated his imagination.

One summer evening as he was going home he heard shouts coming from the direction of a creek nearby. A full scale battle raged and a miner shouted "Help us, Green. Them Tennessee boys are after our claim!" Green headed into the thick of it, grabbed one of the strangers by the arm, whipped him around and dropped him with a blow to the jaw. He dislodged another who had grabbed him from the rear and wheeling about caught him in the belly with his knee. Still holding a piece of Green's shirt in his hand, his attacker tumbled backward into the creek. The fight continued until the Georgians routed the claim jumpers. Green headed for home, his left arm hanging limp, his lip cut and his face badly bruised.

"Look at you! Your face is a sight and that shirt in shreds. You been fighting just like the rest of those no account miners when you've been raised to know better," said his mother, Elizabeth.

"Ma, I heard shouts coming from down near the creek and I went to see what it was about. It was a crowd a Tennessee miners tryin' to take our Georgia boys claim and I had to lay into 'em."

"They were all probably lawless varmints! It was their fight, not yours."

"No, those miners were after one of our claims. That made it my fight, too."

"You're stubborn-willed, Green. What will you be gettin' into next?"

The boy dropped his head for he didn't know. To him some things were right and some were wrong and you chose sides and did what you had to do at the moment. There was a kind of craziness in the air and a mining mania had spread over north Georgia, for anyday could bring instant riches.

Some, but by no means all, of the Indians were reluctantly leaving for Oklahoma. Chief Ross had enough influence to delay the actual removal for several years. Unfortunately, with the delay, the Georgians' frenzy to seize the Cherokee land mounted. It didn't matter that these people could read and write, were Baptists, Methodists or other Christian denominations, for white ministers, too, went along with the move to take the Indian lands. Many Indians could not believe what was happening to them and continued to farm and hunt as they had always done, but President Martin Van Buren was determined to carry out his predecessor's harsh policy of removal.

One day in 1838 a soldier knocked on the Russells' door. He wanted a glass of water from the springhouse. Out in the yard stood others. "Thankee. We're goin' to get rid a these Injuns for you." Green didn't answer and he watched with growing rage as soldiers from all over Georgia entered the Cherokee Nation to track down his Indian friends. They seized them in their homes, allowed them to carry almost nothing with them and herded entire families into stockades to stay until they could round up more for the march west to Oklahoma. In farm areas inaccessible by road soldiers walked along stream beds in order to get back into the coves and hollows and force Indians out of their homes.

People who had drawn a piece of property in the state lottery sometimes stood in the yard ready to move into the house as soldiers with bayonets prodded its Cherokee owners to leave. Across the split rail fences of the fields the Indians had cleared with great labor, hostile white faces stared at them. Families were given minutes to gather whatever they could—clothes, blankets and cook pots—before saying good-bye to their homes forever.

The last view of home many Cherokees had was of seeing white strangers moving their belongings into the house they were being forced at gun point to leave. Every day the soldiers would bring more people into the stockade where rough temporary huts had been built for them to live.

"I'm going to join General Winfield Scott," Green announced one day. His mother and two brothers looked at him in shocked surprise. They were at first bewildered since most of Green's friends were Cherokees.

"Free Jim" who owned a large store in Dahlonega asked why he was going and he told him. "I can help them on the march west," he said briefly. "I don't blame you. It's a cruel way to treat them," said the handsome young man, a mulatto, with skin the color of spun gold.

Not long after Green enlisted he was inside the stockade and spoke to Quatie Ross, wife of Chief John Ross. "Go away! You have become one of them," she said turning her face away angrily as he greeted her.

"I have heard how they humiliated my people in Alabama. Some even killed themselves rather than be paraded through the streets in chains and I will do the same!"

"Hush! That won't change a bad situation, Quatie," said Green.

Two years before when the extensive Creek removal was underway in Alabama, an eighty-four year old woman,

Eneah Emathala, had become the heroine and leader of a group whose only desire was to be allowed to stay and live without harming anyone. "I believe the trip will be orderly and I am going along to do what I can to see that everyone is well treated," he assured her despite some misgivings.

Some of the Cherokees were being transported on steamboats but an officer told Green the group in the stockade was to travel overland. They were to walk across Tennessee, Kentucky, Illinois, and Missouri until they arrived in Arkansas.

When Green rode out with the militia and Indians, the colors of the north Georgia foothills melted together under the warm October sun in a brilliant profusion of red, purple, and gold. Every gust of wind rained down bright showers of color.

"How far must we go?" a frail old Indian woman stopped him to ask, never dreaming the trip would take from three to five months.

"A long, long way," Green replied and spurred his horse, afraid she would read the truth in his eyes. He knew it would be a miracle if she lived to reach Oklahoma. By the time the Indians had walked as far as Illinois, the trees were charcoal silhouettes against a steel gray sky and freezing winds blasted the plains chilling them to the bone.

Green knew Chief Ross had asked that this removal take place later in the season for many had died on the last trip West, due to severe summer heat. But it seemed to him it was too close to winter although he was learning there was no season when the trip could be made without risk. Weather in the Great Plains was harsh and unpredictable any time of year. In Illinois, behind the soldiers on horseback, the ragged, thinly clad Indian families formed an almost endless, ragged column with the sharp wind whipping up the dust around them. Sometimes walking in sleeting rain, sometimes in driving snow, it was a battle of endurance for both Indians and soldiers.

Awake at daybreak each morning, Green heard hungry children crying pitifully, and pots clattering while an effort was made to prepare something edible from the scant supply of food. Officers cursed impatiently as they tried to hurry the unwieldly throng of people. In the years ahead he would hear these sounds in his dreams.

Sometimes, when one of the Indians became too weak or ill to walk and was dying, a member of the family insisted on staying behind, too. At first the militiamen tried to prevent them, but after the soldiers had been on the trail for a while they let the Indians stay with their loved one. The one who stayed behind would sicken and die, or become a renegade, but there was no room in the handful of wagons to carry the sick and no time to wait for them to recover. Those who died quickly were fortunate.

One day Green rode back to check on Chief John Ross's wife and found the women weeping. The weather had been freezing the night before and like many others Quatie had slept on the icy ground. Hearing a child crying she had awakened and spread her own blanket over the little girl. Later that morning Mrs. Ross died from exposure. Green's face turned white and he struggled to control his anger.

Chief John Ross's father was a Scotsman, and he was a literate, educated man by anyone's standards, but because he had some Cherokee blood, he was regarded as Cherokee. Without his beloved Quatie, Chief John Ross would face exile alone. Even his status as Chief did not save his wife from inhuman treatment thought Green as two of the Indian men hurriedly dug a shallow grave beside the trail while the women encircled it. He was not much at public prayer so he read a psalm aloud. They turned to follow the wagons and riders, the cloud of dust hovering over the long, snake-like formation of human misery.

A few of the soldiers tried to help the Cherokees. One wrote of this trip years later saying, "I fought through the Civil War and have seen men shot to pieces and slaughtered by the thousands but the Cherokee Removal was the cruelest work I ever knew." If there was much of the boy in Green when he started, it was gone when he returned to Dahlonega at the end of the trek. After the Cherokees were evicted and their land seized, the mining went smoothly, but beneath the surface lay a great festering bitterness.

Among the Russell family's closest friends were the Willises and the McClures. The grandfathers of both Susan Willis and Frances McClure were half Cherokee and there were many people in the area of mixed heritage. Green had known Susan Willis since he was boy and in 1845, he and Susan were married. Two years later she gave birth to a son whom they named John Randolph, a boy who later would be closer to Green's heart than any of his other seven children.

Green was happy during these years but he became restless. Surface gold in the Dahlonega area was dwindling and the new methods of vein mining required more capital than the average man possessed.

As luck would have it, the wife of a former Georgia man happened to be cooking for Captain Sutter's crew at the time James Marshall found the first particles of gold in Sutter's millrace. When Mrs. Peter Wimmer saw the men test a shining substance by boiling it in her soup kettle, a jet plane couldn't have gotten the news back to Georgia much quicker!

"Did you hear about the letter from Mrs. Wimmer," Jim Boisclair asked Green when he was in the store. It was all Green Russell needed to hear. A few months later the tall, striking man with the jauntily curled mustache and luxuriant brown beard with the two braided plaits, rode out of Dahlonega leading a party of miners West.

The Georgians were experienced and panned in every stream they crossed, seeing a little color now and then, but not stopping for they knew the rich finds lay ahead in California. The route was not uncharted but the maps were sometimes inaccurate. Green decided to strike out upon a northern route rejecting the more direct but dangerous route across the American Desert.

Following the course of the Arkansas River across the great plains, his party turned north and skirted the Rocky Mountains taking the Oregon Trail following the North Platte River to Fort Laramie. Then the Russel group headed westward over the California trail and dropped south into the gold region. They traveled three thousand miles on horseback, by covered wagon, and sometimes on foot.

When Green and his followers finally arrived in San Francisco, everyone was in a state of wild excitement. Hundreds of vessels lay at anchor in the bay and crews were abandoning ship to head for the hills. Crops were left unharvested in the fields. Soldiers deserted and the men sent to capture them deserted, too. But the Georgia miners were at home in the gold rush atmosphere. No amateurs, they could recognize good outcroppings and they knew how to build the rockers, cradles, and longtoms used back home which would greatly increase their production of gold.

Before the Georgians arrived, the only experienced miners were Mexicans from Sonora who had taken part in a small gold rush in 1842 near San Fernando when a hungry rancher took his knife to dig up a clump of wild onions and saw particles of gold clinging to the roots.

The gold discovery of 1849 was in the mineral soil of the western slopes of the "Mother Lode" and gold seekers by the hundreds poured into the area through which Highway 49 runs today. Some traveled the arduous overland route as did the Georgians, while others took the long sea route around Cape Horn. Either journey was hazardous.

By the end of the year Green and John Russell had mined a sufficient amount of gold to head back to Georgia, for Green had promised to return bringing with him his younger brothers. Deciding that they would go back by sea they left San Francisco for Panama City, crossing the Isthmus by canoe and after reaching the Atlantic side, engaged a paddle wheeler to New Orleans. Green wanted to travel by steamer up the Mississippi for he was already considering the river route for his trip back to the gold fields with Oliver and Levi.

At thirty, Green Russell was a seasoned adventurer and leader. Home for a few months that spring, he was ready to head West again by summer with his two brothers and a party of neighbors. Viewing the Mississippi riverboat traffic and the big paddle wheelers for the first time was an experience for these rural Georgians, and in New Orleans they were amazed by the strange food, the melodic sounds of the Creole language, and the docks with ships from exotic places.

"What do we need to take with us," other travelers would ask Green, "and where are the best gold fields?" Oliver and Levi were proud of their big, russet-bearded brother and the respect he received. Green Russell seemed completely free from fear, accepted life as he found it, and

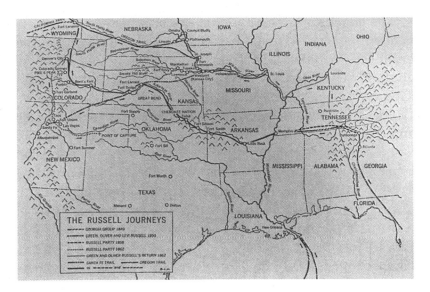

THE RUSSELL JOURNEYS

Elma Dill Russell Spencer, University of Texas
Press, Austin, TX

knew how to get along with people. Levi tried to emulate his
qualities but Oliver, always shy, did not even try to match
him.

When their boat reached Panama they got off at the city
of Chagres and next day climbed into canoes for the trip on
the turgid Chagres River through the isthmus ... then
started out on foot toward the Pacific. Luckily Green secured mules for them to cross the hills of Culebra; and when
they finally reached Panama City they celebrated despite
the crowds and oppressive heat.

Levi and Oliver remembered the disapproving story from
their brother, John, of how on his first trip to Panama City,
Green had met a Mr. King who, because of the throngs of
people, had waited so long for a boat that he had run out of
money. He could neither go on to California nor did he have
funds left to get home.

The generous Green had lent the stranger the money he needed to get to his destination and the grateful man had promised to repay him soon ... but John told them he doubted whether they would ever see the money or Mr. King again.

Boat transportation to California was improved by 1850 and Green and his two brothers booked passage on the S.S. *Oregon*, a Pacific mail carrier. The run from Panama to San Francisco was uneventful and it was a brilliantly sunny day as they sailed into the Golden Gate. Cannon on the ship thundered and while the brothers stood beside the rail waiting to land they could see exhuberant celebrating on shore. The *Oregon* had just brought the news that California had become a state of the Union and everyone was cheering widely. They thrilled to the historic moment.

Pushed and jostled on the dock, confused by a bedlam of voices speaking in foreign languages and surrounded by the faces of people of many races, the brothers found themselves in a sprawling boomtown of tents, shanties, and log houses as far as they could see.

It was hard to get food and when they could find it prices were astronomical. The first night they paid an exorbitant amount for a room in the worst possible section, but luckily, most men looked at the tall, broad-shouldered Green with his reddish beard, braided pirate style in two plaits, and decided to leave the Russells alone.

"If it isn't Green Russell! How are you," said a stranger placing his hand on Green's arm and greeting him warmly. "I'm King, from North Carolina ... the fellow you probably never expected to see again." It was the man Green had loaned money to in Panama and he paid him back immediately and invited the brothers to join him in working his claim north of the Sutter area near Marysville. They laid in provisions and equipment and headed for Marysville working there until, ten thousand dollars better off, Green was ready to move on to the American River region.

Months passed as they prospected at various sites and after two successful years passed in California even Green was thinking about home. The Russells started back by boat. In Havana a pickpocket stole Levi's wallet and with Green shouting "After him," the trio raced through a throng of surprised Latins, caught the unfortunate thief by his guyjara shirt and when he struggled to get away they kicked him with their square-toed boots until he gladly thrust the wallet at them.

It was on the last lap of the trip that tragedy struck, for the ship was scourged with the dread cholera. Many of the men died within three to five days of their first symptoms. Levi was intensely interested in disease and its treatment and while he cautioned his brothers on how to avoid contagion, he himself, constantly ministered to the sick and dying. Green feared the outcome but he could not discourage him and as he and Oliver expected, Levi, too, came down with the disease.

Green's anguish and frustration were similar to his feelings during the march with his Cherokee friends, for there was nothing he could do nor did doctors have a remedy. Treatment for cholera was to deny the patient fresh water, but Levi did not think that made sense and when everyone was asleep he would drag himself weakly from his bed each night and down to a water barrel. There he would remain with his feverish face resting in the cool water, drinking his fill.

When the Russell brothers reached Key West, crew and passengers were placed in quarantine. The sun beat down upon them day after day as the ship rocked monotonously to

and fro and people died around them. Levi was one of those
fortunate enough to recover and he attributed it to his
nightly trips to the water barrel. Green, by some great good
fortune immune to the disease, paced the deck, sketched
maps of the West from memory for the future and thought
about the long trip across Florida to Georgia. Finally, they
were released from quarantine and began the journey
home.

News of the Russell brothers' return reached Dahlonega
ahead of them and on their arrival townspeople and others
from the surrounding area were waiting to hear about the
trip from Green Russell.

At last, Green seemed ready to settle down and he purchased Savannah Plantation, the Palmer property near
Hightower, for ten thousand dollars. It was a beautiful place
of about five hundred acres with a cluster of houses on a
small rise overlooking a green valley and at the foot of the
rise was a swift flowing brook that became known as Russell Creek. Here Green and Susan brought his mother, Elizabeth, and his brothers and sisters.

It was 1855 and Elizabeth Russell had not been strong for
several years, but she managed to live through her favorite
season of the year—spring in the Georgia foothills—and
then she died. She was buried at Savannah Plantation almost within sight of the house. Oliver was to be married in
June but there is a time for grief and a time for joy and
everyone agreed that the wedding should be postponed
until fall. Vivacious "Sukie," Green's wife, was now head of
the household, and in September she gave a party for
Oliver's fiancée, Jane.

The Russells were a music-loving, dancing folk and the
celebration was an exuberant one, but poor Baptist Jane
languished on the sidelines unable to dance while the

groom frolicked past with everyone else. She decided that night that her children would learn to dance when they learned to walk!

Another house was added to the cluster on the hill when Levi, coming home to Dahlonega from medical school to practice, married Mary Roe. Green had thought they would all continue mining there at home for there was still gold in north Georgia, but they decided farming and land were more stable. Some men would have first considered land in Georgia but not Green Russell. There was new land to be had, land opening up in the Kansas Territory, and he and Oliver decided to go.

Although it was utterly unlike Georgia, this flat, vast expanse of plains that stretched mile upon mile to the edge of the horizon, the two brothers found acreage to their liking in Pottawatomie County and staked out claims for a farm.

But it was not long before Green's thoughts returned to gold. He couldn't forget the half-breed Baptist preacher named John Beck who had been part of the Cherokee group headed by Lewis Ralston seven years before. They had found a small showing of gold in the Rocky Mountains on the way to California and Green had heard they had made a map of the location. He wrote Beck who agreed to form a party of Cherokees with the Russells while Green and Oliver recruited Georgia prospectors.

In the meantime military forces thought the threat from hostile Western Indians too dangerous for an immediate trip and advised them to wait a year. Reluctantly, Green decided his party would wait and join forces with the Cherokees in the spring of 1858. Just planning to head West again made him feel more alive. He was convinced that the greatest adventure of all lay before him. What drives men to travel thousands of miles by wagon or on foot across un-

charted wilderness country, risk freezing to death or dying
of thirst, in a journey that could prove futile? What drives a
man like Green Russell?

Anticipation was mingled with sadness at Savannah
Plantation that winter as the brothers prepared for the trip.
Levi had decided to go, too, despite the protests of his bride
of a few months and other men from the neighborhood were
joining them—Lewis Ralston, William Anderson, Joseph
McAfee, Solomon Roe, Samuel Bates, and John Hampton.

Dawn on the morning of February 17, 1858, was crisp and
cold and Suki watched her husband's breath . . . a white
curling mist in the air . . . as she hugged him in the yard
before he left. Then he climbed into the wagon and in a few
minutes she heard the sound of the men's voices and their
teams float back across the woods from the "Old Gold
Diggers Road" as they headed toward Dahlonega four miles
away. By sundown their heavy mule drawn wagons were
creaking along a mountain trail.

After weeks of travel, they reached Marysville in Indian
Territory but the Indians were not yet ready to come. A later
date was set to meet at the Big Bend of the Arkansas River
and they went on to Kansas. They were joined at Green's
farm on Rock Creek by the Pierce boys from Dahlonega and
three men from the Kansas Territory. One of these, Luke
Tierney, planned to keep a trip log. More prospectors joined
them and exchanging mule teams for oxen at Leavenworth
they set off, now numbering twenty-one.

There were four wagons, ten yoke of oxen and three
horses, which Green considered about the right number to
meet any trials or dangers. At Fort Riley they lost time
recovering some animals that had strayed and the river
crossing was treacherous but every wagon made it. Game
was scarce until they reached the Santa Fe Trail and from

then on buffalo was their main supply of fresh meat. Daytime heat was so oppressive that Green decided they would travel by night.

On June second his company joined the Cherokees and together they made up seventy men, fourteen wagons, thirty-three yoke of cattle, two horse teams and twenty or more ponies. This gave them protection against attack and members of both parties were heartened.

Beck was the organizer of the Cherokees but they were under the command of a former Cherokee chief, a lawyer named George Hicks, and had to obey his rules of travel. There would be no Sunday marches unless unavoidable for Hicks believed that a Sabbath rest was needed by both men and cattle. His party consisted of thirty Cherokees, a few white men, two of whom had brought their wives, Mrs. Kelly and Mrs. Kirk, as well as Mrs. Kelly's sister and the Kirk children.

Watching the backs of the oxen swaying rhythmically as they moved down the trail ahead of him, Green had time to think because for the time being there was less leadership responsibility and the way along the river was familiar. He began to wish he had brought his wife, Sukie, when he glanced over at Mrs. Kelly and Mrs. Kirk. On June 18 the wagons left the Arkansas River behind and turned north toward the mountains.

The road now rose steadily and they could see snow-topped Pike's Peak to the northwest in the splendor of the sunset. Still some thirty miles away, it seemed much nearer in the deceptively clear, mountain air. Green would be drawn forever by the beauty of this country where verdant green slopes were in bright contrast to snow-covered mountain summits.

On they went passing one abandoned camp site after another. A rock five hundred feet high loomed grimly above them on the trail and at its base stood a small wooden cross inscribed: "Charles Michael Fagan—1858." "He's been dead only a short time," said Green hoping the poor fellow's end whether from illness, Indians, or some renegade's gun had come quickly.

After the wagons had bumped and sloughed and strained across interminable miles of plains they stopped near Cherry Creek, a small stream emptying into the Platte River. The following morning the sun was warm on Green's shoulders as he watched one of the men wade into the stream and pan gravel. He saw several particles of gold in the pan but was not impressed for the real object of the prospecting expedition was Ralston's Creek. They arrived there just before nightfall of June 24. If they expected to find placer gold thick as hailstones, it certainly wasn't visible and the more inexperienced miners were the first to become discouraged.

Then the Cherokees became restless and eager to leave, not so much over failure to find gold quickly, but for fear of Western Indians. They had urged Green to build a fort ever since they arrived, but he planned no permanent settlement for he did not anticipate any real danger. The area had not been prospected, they had ample provisions, and Green felt this was a second chance at gold for the Cherokees since they had gained nothing but misery from the Georgia gold. The Cherokees, however, did not want another chance.

They were apprehensive about hostile tribes and to them the Great American desert was an awesome, perilous region awakening all their deepest superstitions and uneasiness. There wasn't anything about this part of the country the Indians liked and on Sunday, the fourth of July, Green was deserted by both Cherokees and whites. Of 104 men only 30 remained.

Two days later when the prospectors who had stayed were crossing a river, a wagon with their most important supplies overturned in mid-stream. They got into the water and were able to rescue almost everything except their matches. They were miles from nowhere. The fire that night had to be lit from the sparks of flints struck together and the men were greatly disheartened. More gave up, and as they prepared to leave Green faced the deserting prospectors.

"Gentlemen, you can all go but I will stay if only two men will stay with me. I will remain to satisfy myself that no gold can be found."

His two brothers and ten other men stayed. Now, there was Sam Bates, the Pierce boys, and Solomon Roe from Georgia; Luke Tierney, Jacob Masterson, and Theodore Herring of Kansas Territory; Valarious Young of Iowa; William McFadding of North Carolina; and William McKimens of Pennsylvania. In just three days, ninety-one men had turned their backs on the opportunity of a lifetime.

The little party of thirteen started up the Platte River toward the mountains. That afternoon at Cherry Creek, only eight miles from their start that morning, young Jim Pierce lagged behind the wagons to pan some gravel. Since Jim was the least experience, Green finished washing out the contents of his pan for him and it contained the finest gold they had seen.

They were now in the region of the Rockies called the Pike's Peak area. Here they pitched camp for the next few months and prospected.

Sometimes they had a visitor who would stay for a day or two and pan with them and Green had no idea of the

They stopped and panned at every stream looking for color.
Harper's New Monthly Magazine, 1858

exaggerated reports that were spreading about their gold finds. So far they had found only drift gold, and he knew they must head further into the mountains to find the rich veins. The little band of prospectors intended to determine the location of the deposits for future development and for this reason they never mined in the same place at the same time.

They spread out but not any great distance from one another for there was always the possibility of danger from Indians, although, sometimes for an entire month at a time, they saw no other human beings. When their provisions ran out they lived on wild game—bear, elk, mountain sheep, and one night there was even wildcat for supper . . . they ate whatever they could find.

By late summer they were on their way back to the placer camp region. Green was convinced that great deposits of gold lay in the Rockies and calling his men together he proposed that since winter was close upon them, they return to Georgia, round up supplies and plan a trip in the spring deeper into the Rockies. They would take most of the gold dust they had back to Georgia to the Dahlonega Mint to exchange for money. Levi was to stay behind in charge of the winter camp.

He was the youngest and Green and Oliver were not happy at the prospect of leaving him there with so much responsibility; but he and his men could do a little prospecting and if Levi ran out of provisions he could always sell his gold watch at Fort Garland, Colorado. A timepiece was not important in the wilderness where men's activities were based on the rising and setting sun.

Taking only two men with him, the "Russell boys," a term often applied to the men under Green's leadership, started on their six hundred mile trip east across the plains. The three riders had only one blanket each and the weather was unpredictable. They had no pack animal to carry provisions and were limited to game they could find along the way. Even firewood was scarce at times as there were few trees on the plains away from the river banks. One night wolves devoured the camp supplies and drove off their pony and mules. Now, there was nothing left, only a little coffee for three men.

They rode all that day without food, their situation growing more and more serious. There was no sign of game nor travelers to help them. Finally, in the distance, they sighted a wagon . . . a group of Dutch emigrants making camp and Oliver Russell helped them start their fire. The emigrants reluctantly sold them a few morsels of food but would not even let them use their fire to cook it. The next day they were still without food but were fortunate enough to meet some soldiers far more generous who gave them food and fed their horses for them. But they were still a long way from Leavenworth, Kansas.

The three riders were amazed to begin meeting so many heading West. These groups would be facing dangerous winter weather soon but none would heed their warnings. Near Bent's Fort, on the Arkansas River, the Russells met the wagon train of the Larimer group from Leavenworth who said they were bound for Pike's Peak. Had he seen them sooner, Green told them, he would have advised they wait until spring, for the winter blizzards would soon be upon them. They continued to meet more and more travelers. Several stopped to trade news saying they had heard about a fabulous strike in the Rockies made by some men named Russell who had found gold everywhere.

It was useless to tell these would-be prospectors that the gold thus far did not justify the hope of easy mining, that it was the most dangerous time of the year, that there were no shelters built along the way against the cold and snow, and no place to obtain food or equipment any closer than the towns from which they had come! When they were almost home the Russells discovered that it was a man named John Cantrell with a little sack of gold dust, panned on a visit to them and carried back East, who had ignited this nation-wide excitement.

In 1858 newspaper headlines were screaming "GOLD IN KANSAS TERRITORY!! AND THE PIKE'S PEAK MINES!! Gold had been discovered again in the West and this time nearer than California . . . carried by word of mouth, each report more exaggerated than the last. Cantrell's appearance and talk of gold the year after the depression of

1857 was all desperate people needed to go wild. No one wanted to be bothered with the facts. Plows were left in the fields, businesses padlocked, and homesites deserted. The gold stampede was on!

After two years absence, Oliver and Green each saw their new sons for the first time. Sadly enough, Levi's little boy, Charlie, had died a few weeks earlier and there was sorrow among the cluster of houses at Savannah Plantation. But life went on, for it was Christmas and everyone tried to make it as happy a one as possible.

Green took the gold to the Dahlonega Mint and it was the first Rocky Mountain gold to be minted. He was famous now and people came from miles around to see him. When it was known that he would be taking another party west in the spring he was besieged by men wanting to join him. Tom Stowers who couldn't go, offered to finance those who could. Stowers, like Dahlonega's colorful Jim Boisclair, had done this for prospectors going to California in 1849.

Returning to the foothills of the Rockies that spring Green was astonished to find Cherry Creek now a thriving settlement and he named it Auraria after his birthplace in Georgia. Across the creek, another settlement sprang up and the entire area would someday be known as Denver. Near the present site of Black Hawk and Central City in the mountains west of Denver, his fellow Georgian, John Gregory, discovered the celebrated vein that became known as the Gregory Lode. Georgia pioneers had contributed to Colorado's rapid settlement and brought about its statehood just seventeen years later.

With the outbreak of the Civil War, the situation of the Southerners grew tense in Colorado. Green and Oliver had intended to stay there until the war ended but were now

ready to leave Denver, for they were tired of the insults
being heaped upon Southerners.

The Russell group decided to go back to Georgia and
wanted to take a route with as little danger of meeting
Union soldiers as possible. Green thought they should go by
way of California Gulch under the guise of prospectors
traveling from there down through New Mexico. There
would be eighteen of them in all and they would be carrying
about twenty-thousand dollars in gold.

"We've crossed these plains together and been all over
this country without dreading Indians," said Green, "and
now we are disguising ourselves for fear of white men!"

They couldn't tell anyone they wanted to go home but
had to steal their way through military lines. They passed
through the San Luis Valley and on to Fort Garland and
from there they made it safely to Taos, then north to Las
Vegas. At Las Vegas, Green learned that a company of
soldiers had just gone down to the Pecos to set up camp at
the river's headwaters in order to prevent any parties from
going south. Green believed that their only alternative now
was the Santa Fe Road to Fort Smith, Arkansas. As they
headed in that direction they were just one day behind the
soldiers and their tracks were still fresh. But disaster had
already struck.

In Taos a man by the name of Ike Roberts who knew a few
of the Russell party had asked to go along with them saying
he was broke. Green did not trust his character nor did
several others but he was taken in anyway. It was a tragic
mistake. In four days the man broke out with smallpox. The
group was out in the middle of the plains with provisions
that would last only a short time and men coming down
with smallpox. There was no way to stop and Green ordered
the party on, although about half the company were ill and

several would soon die. Levi, the only doctor in the party, had no vaccine and could only use the medicine he had with him to treat the disease after its onset.

They had traveled two or three hundred miles on the Forth Smith Road when Green looked up from his breakfast one morning to see two Indians coming into camp.

"Our village is nearby and the chief sent us to talk with you and find out who you are and what you are doing here in Comanche country?" He spoke good English Green observed.

"We're prospectors," he replied briefly and with that the two men left, but the Russells were suspicious.

Green was in the lead wagon and when the party approached the place where they expected to find the Indian village he saw a startling sight. About a quarter of a mile away on the hill facing them were mounted Indian warriors dressed in war plumes and armed with guns, bows, and spears. He had only seventeen men and six lay sick in the wagons. Pierce, Rippey, and Odum were riding a little ahead of the wagons and at that point, just opposite the mouth of a large ravine where they were about to wait to confer with the other men, a voice cried out in English, "Halt!"

They looked up the ravine and saw soldiers ... their muskets and revolvers all leveled and cocked. "Surrender, or you are dead men," an officer shouted. Green Russell asked only one question, "To whom are we surrendering?" The reply came back, "To Lieutenant Shoop, commanding United States Cavalry."

"We surrender," called out Green relieved because of the Indians and the smallpox epidemic. He had no idea that he was surrendering to an alliance of U.S. Troops and Indians. The Cavalry had told the Indians that the group they were pursuing were Texas Rangers in the Confederate Army, and if they would help capture them they would receive one of the men to torture!

"I could have intercepted you a hundred and fifty miles back but what we really thought was that you were a band of guerillas from New Mexico under a desperado named Madison," said Shoop.

"Well, we aren't," replied Green angrily.

When the officer found out the Russell group were pioneers of Colorado and everybody knew each other—some of the privates had even worked for Green in Russell Gulch—he regretted making the agreement with the Indians.

But, of course, the arrangement had already been made with the Indians and they were demanding that their cruel contract be fulfilled. Green and his men had been disarmed, half were sick, and they were surrounded by a thousand Indian warriors claiming a victim. Their situation was desperate.

Meanwhile, Shoop had gotten the chiefs together to explain that he had made a mistake and these were not the Rangers. But the Indians had been promised guns, horses, and provisions and now they felt cheated; sounds from the Indian camp at night were ominous and each man of the Russell group who was healthy enough to know what was happening wondered whether it would be he. Green would have offered himself to save his men, but efforts to appease the Indians were still going on and he waited for the outcome. It was hard to think clearly now for stricken with smallpox himself, he was soon to be one of the sickest.

Among the soldiers under Shoop was the American agent to the Comanchees, a man named Stapp. He talked with the Indians at great length telling them their annuities were at government headquarters and threatening that they would not receive them if they attempted to take any man by force. In desperation, he promised them extra presents. Muttering angrily the Indians began to break camp and leave. Stapp went with them himself for three days to insure that they did not change their minds and return. Stapp's threats and promises were all that saved one of the group from having to be given up to the Comanchees.

After the Indians left the Russell group was taken as prisoners to Fort Union and a few days later were placed on parole with freedom to go anywhere within four miles of the fort. The food was good, they had kind treatment and comfortable quarters. There were no charges against them other than their wanting to go home to Georgia. Their gold was being held along with their horses and other possessions.

Finally, after taking the oath of allegiance to the United States, they were released and the gold and their horses returned to them. Green and Oliver headed for Georgia, taking the oath at every point where Union troops stopped them nor did they violate it. Finally they got home and stayed in Georgia until the war was over.

Green had some claims left in the West and he decided to take his family to the Rocky Mountain country. On October 20, 1871, shortly after their arrival, he settled in the Greenhorn mountains section, which offered wild game, water and grass for cattle, and also seemed likely for gold prospecting. Several years went by and Green was once more prospering in mining when in the fall of 1874 his son, John Randolph, was killed in a mine accident.

From then on he lost heart. The area reminded him of John and he and Sukie decided to move to a place he had always loved, the Sangre de Cristo Mountains about ten miles from Fort Garland. But in Colorado he was also reminded of John. After visiting his brother and his wife's sister-in-law, Frances, who had settled in the Cherokee Nation, they decided to move to the Nation permanently to a place on the Canadian River near Briartown.

Green looked forward to the move. He had always talked about how he loved to see crops growing and that gold had been chiefly a means to acquire land. This period was one he had anticipated as a time of contentment and for a while it was just as he had dreamed it would be. He planted cotton, corn, and wheat, and his crops thrived. Then malaria struck in June of 1877 and Sukie was first to be prostrated with violent chills and fever.

At one time not a single member of the family was able to wait upon another and neighbors came in to take care of them. In mid-August Green was much better and went out in the yard ... there to suffer a convulsion. Good doctors were scarce in that part of the country and there was no one to treat him. Within ten days he was dead. Levi Russell was to always regret that he had not been with him, for he believed he might have saved his brother's life.

Green was three years under sixty and as healthy and strong as most men of forty. When news of his death went out it was not only his family but many others who mourned him, for scattered throughout the country were people he had helped and men who had followed him on his expeditions. However desperate the situation, no one had ever seen Green show fear. He had the love of his family and the respect of Cherokees and whites. By now, Southerners were scattered throughout the western and southwestern states. Oliver became a rancher in Mendardville, Texas, and Levi settled there, also, practicing medicine.

But Green Russell, one of the towering figures of both the southern and western gold rushes, was gone, and never

again on this earth would any man hear his compelling
voice and follow where the calm, broad-shouldered, fear-
less man with the plaited russet beard led.

There are probably many people who are unaware that a
Georgian laid the foundation of a great western state, Colorado. Below is an excerpt from a letter from the State Histo-
rian of Colorado, L. R. Hafen, in Denver to County His-
torian, A. W. Cain of Dahlonega, Georgia in 1931.

Dear Mr. Cain:
". . . Yes, our early history has a close connection with
Auraria, Georgia. The important pioneer prospecting party
that discovered gold in the region of the present Colorado
was formed in Auraria, Georgia, by W. G. Russell, his two
brothers, and other relatives and friends. They left Georgia
in February, 1858 and came to the present site of Denver.
They discovered some gold in this vicinity and it was stories
of these finds that inaugurated the famous Pikes Peak gold
rush of 1859 and laid the foundation of Colorado. The
Russell party founded the first settlement at the present site
of Denver, and named it Auraria in honor of their home
town. A month later the town of Denver started on the
opposite side of Cherry Creek. In April, 1860, the two settle-
ments were consolidated under the name of Denver."

18.
Darling of the Gold Camps

In the spring of 1853 tall, brown-haired Mary Ann Crabtree, of the schoolmarm, ramrod carriage, and her five-year-old daughter, Lotta, set out from the port of New York to San Francisco. They braved storms at sea, outbreaks of cholera, bandits, and the discomforts of a tiny boat on the River Chagres across the Isthmus of Panama all to join Mrs. Crabtree's husband, a doctor, who had set out to make his fortune in the gold fields.

Journeying up the coast of California, the intrepid Mary Ann and her little girl finally arrived at the city the whole world was talking about.

When their small ship docked in San Francisco, fog was rolling in from the bay wrapping itself around the tents, shanties, and log buildings giving the whole scene, so unlike any city to them, the appearance of a landscape in a bad dream. It was a dismal, disappointing arrival. Carrying their suitcases, mother and daughter climbed the slippery stone steps leading up to the wharf at Pacific and Davis Streets and began to walk along Pacific Street among the auction marts piled high with jewelry and clothing, staring wide-eyed at dance halls, cheap saloons, and dives, all teeming with sailors, miners, prostitutes, gamblers, and assorted disreputable characters.

They heard the strains of loud piano music, squeaky fiddles, blaring trombones, and rowdy voices in this area bounded on the east by the waterfront, the west by Chinatown, and the north by Broadway.

Mr. Crabtree was not there to meet his wife and daughter but a message was waiting saying he would write soon and was "somewhere in the mountains."

Fortunately, they had friends to stay with, but the sights they showed Mary Ann, although dazzling ones, outraged her puritanical views. It was a mindboggling mixture, for although saloons and gambling halls abounded, good theater was also plentiful. In 1853 the roughest miners could take their choice of performances by the world's most famous actors and actresses of the day. There were farces and burlesques, song and dance acts, English comedies, and Shakespearian dramas.

Mrs. Crabtree found herself viewing an exciting whirlpool of dramatic talent unlike anything she had ever seen before even in New York. While she was absorbing all of this and enjoying much of it, despite her disapproval, a letter arrived from husband, John.

"So far I have been cursed by ill luck although I shall not go into all the wretched details at this time that have befallen a man of my integrity and diligence. However, a magnificent idea has occurred to me which I am convinced will make our fortune.

"In the meantime, living conditions here have been far from comfortable for me. I desire that you and Lotta set out at once to join me in Grass Valley. This is the Mecca of the mining world. While the details of my plan are working out, you should find it well within those admirable talents of yours to run a boardinghouse here. There are all kinds of people in this fast growing place that need to be housed and fed."

Mary Ann Crabtree stared thoughtfully at the letter in her hand. She was a practical woman and she knew that by this means she could make a living for herself and Lotta, and in the meantime, John's mine might pan out. She had no way of knowing how events there were to change all of their lives.

Grass Valley was some distance north of the mother lode and as the stage pulled in, Mary Ann saw a picturesque mountain community.

Grass Valley was a rowdy mining town, typically western with its row of connected wooden stores on either side, an overhanging roof to protect pedestrians on the board side-walks from weather, and a muddy thoroughfare down the middle. It did not take Mary Ann long to make a place for herself and "Mrs. Crabtree's" was soon a popular boarding-house not only for visitors but miners, as well.

Lying on the edge of town were the Empire Mine, the Gold Center, the North Star, and other smaller ventures. Returning from a trip to London, General John C. Fremont had brought over Cornish miners. In the earlier gold rushes of the Carolinas and Georgia, the Cornish had proven them-selves adept at getting gold from the hard rock shafts and that was the problem here in Grass Valley. The Cornishmen looked at placer miners contemptuously saying, "They are farmers, not miners."

Too young to be of much help to her mother, Lotta spent her days making friends with the miners and took a particu-lar fancy to the Cornishmen with their colorful speech. One was Jonathon Moyle who often sang the old Christmas carols to her for he was a member of the Grass Valley Cornish Choir. Sometimes, she would join him in the carols and her voice, sweet as the trill of a bird, drew the rough men in hushed silence around her.

Of an evening Jonathon would sit swinging his heavy-booted feet from the porch of the Crabtree house entertaining Lotta with stories of Cornish beliefs about gnomes and leprechauns. Sometimes he talked of elflike Tommy-knockers.

"But what are Tommyknockers, Jonathon?"

"Why, a Tommyknocker is a little fellow who makes the mines safe by doing repairs between shifts and who taps on the timbers to warn a man when a cave-in's coming. You see, they came 'ere with us from the mines in Cornwall."

"I worry about cave-ins sometimes, Jonathon. You work down there so deep under the ground. Are you sure the Tommyknockers will take care of you?"

"Take care of me? Without a doubt. Those little fellows have the best interests of the miners at 'eart, so stop your worrying, now."

Lotta was comforted and the pair began to sing one of the carols at first lustily and then growing softer and softer until it sounded as if their voices were coming from a great distance. Lotta noticed that Jonathon's large gray eyes were moist and impulsively she placed her hand upon his large one.

"Are you sad, Jonathon?"

"Now and then when I think of them I left behind me in Cornwall." The grizzled miner gave a deep sigh and they sat quietly for a while looking off toward the mountains. But in a moment Lotta's mood changed.

"Then I shall cheer you up by doing a jig for you!" Flinging out her arms comically, she began whirling around him humming her own accompaniment and the big fellow began to smile in spite of himself at the antics of this exuberant little red-haired girl so like an elf herself.

Lotta and her mother had been in the community scarcely a month when ripples of excitement swept Grass Valley. Attracted by the international fame of this flamboy-

ant mining town, the Countess of Lansfeld was coming from
Europe. Townspeople were breathless with anticipation for
all knew who "the Countess" was and that she was none
other than the notorious Lola Montez, an adventuress risen
from music hall dancer to become paramour of King Louis I
of Bavaria. The resulting scandal had caused a revolution
and lost Louis both his throne and the lady. Now, this bold
woman Lola Montez, was arriving in Grass Valley!

Leading her pet bear on a silver chain along the wooden
sidewalk Lola Montez made her first dramatic appearance
in Grass Valley. She wore the most daring gown imaginable
and with her was her new husband, Patrick Purdy Hull who
carried a hamper of champagne. She and Hull bought a
house on Mill Street which was only a few doors from the
Crabtree house.

"Mother, have you seen the beautiful Countess who has
just moved to town?" Six-year-old Lotta was breathless. She
had run all the way from the stores on Main Street where
Lola, dressed in the most elegant attire, was window shop-
ping, fully aware of the sensation she was causing.

Flair described this woman's dancing, fair, her talents as
an actress, but she herself was spectacular. Lola Montez's
presence and sense of the dramatic had made her an overnight sensation in London.

"I've heard about her, replied Mary Ann shaking her
head contemptuously. "Countess, indeed! She is better
known as Lola Montez and even that, I'm afraid, is not her
real name. But . . . after all, she is our neighbor and I think it
is my duty to pay her a call."

"Oh, mother, may I go, may I go," pleaded Lotta, surprised but delighted by her mother's decision to call upon
the Countess and quick to press for a closer look at such an
exotic creature. She swept and dusted so that her mother

would not refuse her and then dressed herself in her best frock. Mary Ann Crabtree would have protested but Lotta was a vision to behold with her red curls and white dress and she was proud of her. What harm could it possibly do the child?

A few minutes later Mrs. Crabtree was knocking upon the door of the house as Lotta stood beside her tingling with anticipation—nor was she to be disappointed. When the door opened her eager gaze took in the most glamorous woman she had ever seen.

The Countess wore a golden yellow silk gown with an immense skirt and tiny waist. Her smooth white shoulders emerged from the folds of soft black lace adorning the bodice like the wings of some exquisite butterfly. And what a face! Jet black hair was parted in the middle and worn full at the sides to frame a perfect oval.

Her skin was alabaster, her red lips curved voluptuously and the enormous dark eyes at once limpid and sultry took in Mary Ann Crabtree with one darting glance and then rested upon Lotta who stared back as if mesmerized. The fragrance of roses followed this magnetic woman bearing Mrs. Crabtree and Lotta into the parlor in her wake.

"Why, good afternoon, ladies," said the Countess including Lotta in this flattering salutation. "You are my first visitors. Please come in," and with a graceful sweep of her hand, she welcomed them into her parlor. It reminded Lotta of a room she had seen in one of the plays in San Francisco. There was furniture with crimson upholstery, gleaming dark wood, a rich-hued Oriental rug, handsome vases, and gleaming brass candelabra with sparkling crystal prisms.

Lola excused herself for a moment and then brought in an elegant Bavarian tea set with gold trim and handpainted yellow roses. Both mother and daughter were so awed they could scarcely answer this glamorous woman's pleasant-ries. It was Lotta who recovered herself first and with her engaging sincerity began to charm the beautiful Lola.

"Everyone is saying you were a great success in San Francisco and that of all the performers . . . you are the favorite of the gold camps."

Lola smiled, "Is that really what they say?"

"Oh, yes. I only wish I could have seen you so I might learn to dance as you do."

"You may, child. You may, indeed, someday. She is a lovely little girl," said Lola turning to Mary Ann Crabtree. "Does she have talent?"

"You would have to judge for I know little of such things," said Mary Ann looking down . . . her small work-worn hands fluttering nervously like California quail in her lap, but she was pleased. Surprisingly, perhaps, because they were so different, Lola and Mary Ann liked each other. The friendship that sprang up that day between the rigidly conventional Mrs. Crabtree and the magnificently flamboy-ant Lola defied explanation.

When the women of the town gossiped or were sus-picious, Mary Ann Crabtree became her defender and when her six-year-old Lotta began to spend whole days with Lola Montez, she trusted her.

Passersby could hear music emanating from the little house hour after hour as Lola taught the child dance rou-tines, songs or bits from plays and the adoring Lotta was quick to learn. She began to sing and dance for Lola's famous visitors from all over the world.

It was an exciting life for Lotta as the home of the Count-ess overflowed with touring theater people, singers, musi-cians, writers, painters, and poets. The extraordinary Stephen Massett, singer and lecturer, visited and even Victor Hugo's two legendary nephews, who came to California to try their luck in the gold mines, dropped by. They fed Lola's exotic collection of parrots, bears, and monkeys and entire parties of her guests would ride out on nearby mountain trails under the blue California skies.

Evenings were spent telling stories, singing, dancing, and playing instruments and the impressionable child learned from it all. When the lovely, dark-eyed little Lotta with her red-gold hair abandoned herself in a rousing Highland fling or Montez version of a gypsy dance, Lola's guests applauded warmly.

"Lotta must go to Paris to study. She is going to be a great actress when she grows up," said Lola and Mary Ann Crabtree was beginning to agree. Two years passed while Lola lived a more "quiet" life than had ever been her custom, shining as hostess and leader of her salon and continuing to train Lotta.

Lotta was learning how to entertain and charm an audience and her mother realized that her love for dance steps and songs was no passing fancy, for each day her skills improved.

But tragedy struck that summer with a cave-in at the mine where Jonathon Moyle worked. Moyle with a great lunge pushed a young miner out of danger but was himself trapped. Lotta spent long hours sitting near the entrance to the mine while the rescue crew worked, but by the end of the third day she was so exhausted from crying that her mother put the heartbroken child to bed.

"Mother, where were the Tommyknockers? Where were they?" asked Lotta over and over. The week of the mine accident John Crabtree, filled with the conviction that it was his destiny to find incredibly rich gold fields higher in the hills, decided they must leave Grass Valley immedi-

Cave-ins were an ever-present danger in underground mines like this one where the Cornishman, Jonathon Moyle, worked.
Harper's New Monthly Magazine, 1858

ately, bag and baggage, for the raw gold camp of Rabbit Creek.

Lotta bade her dear friend, Lola, a tearful good-bye and Lola invited them to stay with her, but by now a new baby had arrived and Mary Ann felt she had no alternative but to dutifully follow her husband. John Crabtree was right. There was gold in Rabbit Creek . . . but not for him. Mary Ann was beginning to discover that her husband was not a man to stick to anything and by the spring of 1855, she was once more running a boardinghouse.

Meanwhile a young Italian whose name had been anglicized to Mart Taylor had come to Rabbit Creek and been so taken with Lotta that he was teaching her more songs and dance steps. She performed at some of the miner's functions and was received with cheers, stamping feet, and hats tossed wildly into the air.

They had been in Rabbit Creek long enough for the mountains slopes to turn deep green from the winter rains when one afternoon Mary Ann heard the sound of a carriage followed by the staccato tap of feminine high heels on the front porch.

"Mary Ann, Mary Ann. Where are you?"

There stood Lola Montez and the two women embraced amid laughter and tears. Lola hugged Lotta with delight. "Come away with me? We will sing! We will dance and you'll be a star!"

"I will! I will! Oh, mother, you'll let me go won't you?" entreated the child, dancing her mother around the porch.

Lola Montez confessed that a vast ennui with country life had overtaken her and she had gone to the trouble of riding up through the hills into the rough country of Rabbit Creek to offer young Lotta the opportunity of a lifetime.

"I have arranged a tour of Australia and I should like for Lotta to come with me."

"Lola, I am truly sorry, but I don't think she should go."

Both the child and the woman used all their powers of persuasion to change her mind; but for reasons scarcely known to herself the adamant Mary Ann refused.

"I wish you luck, Lola, but Lotta must stay here."

Lola turned to wave a last good-bye from her carriage and as she did, Lotta burst into tears and stood on the porch of the house crying as if her heart would break.

Watching the almost equally dispirited Lola ride back down the mountain, Mary Ann wondered, had she been wise? Was she doing the right thing? She wrung her hands on her rough floursack apron with a sense of terrible dismay and uncertainty. Such a chance for her daughter could scarcely come again.

For months Lotta was sad. She knew, now, that she wanted to entertain others and her great opportunity for stardom had probably passed. The stages of the world could have been hers, if her mother had not insisted on keeping her here in a place like this . . . but even in her most bitter hours of disappointment she could still lose herself as she practiced the songs and dances Lola and Mart Taylor taught her. If the world was never to know her, she could still be the star of Rabbit Creek.

One morning when Lotta had gone to the store for her mother, she met Taylor with a stranger, a Dr. Robinson whom Taylor introduced as a producer from San Francisco and, indeed, he was one of the great producers of the day. Robinson had already heard of little Lotta Crabtree from miners in the area.

She was enormously attractive with her reddish hair, sparkling black eyes and adorable smile. Although she was eight years old, she looked much younger and at that time children on the stage were very much in vogue. Best of all, the appealing Lotta genuinely loved her audiences and she knew how to make them like her . . . but, at the moment, there was no opening. Dr. Robinson had Sue Robinson, another child actress, in his company and his meeting with Mart Taylor was to engage Taylor's hall which was the best in town for his young performer.

When Taylor quoted his price, Robinson thought it was entirely too high and he bluntly said "You can keep your hall for I'm going to rent the dance hall across the street!"

Angry, Taylor decided he would teach the Doctor a lesson. Let this important man from San Francisco spotlight his Sue Robinson, he would announce a show of his own on the same night with Lotta Crabtree as his star.

But Robinson was a clever promoter and he called upon Mrs. Crabtree the first evening he was there offering to have Lotta perform several minor numbers during his show, for he was visibly impressed with her engaging ways. Mary Ann asked the important man for time to think about it.

"I'm sorry," she said when he returned for her answer the next day. "I know this is a great opportunity for Lotta but I think her loyalty should go to the man who has helped her first, Mr. Taylor." Robinson inclined his head politely and with only a trace of gruffness in his voice, left. Would little Lotta of Rabbit Creek entice the miners in from the outlying gold camps and outdraw the child star of Dr. Robinson's?

The decision had been made but what was to be done at the last minute to provide the elaborate outfits that would enhance Lotta's acts? Robinson had trunks of ready-made dresses of sequins and peau de soir, muslins with bright silk sashes and lavish satin bows. Lotta Crabtree had none.

Now, the most hectic preparations began for Taylor's show the next evening. Mary Ann sewed feverishly on an adorable green jacket, breeches, and tall hat. Taylor brought out his whittling knife and carved out a shillalah and a pair of comic brogans to complete an Irish costume. But Lotta's mother was not satisfied that this was enough and she set to work sewing all night on an angelic white dress for a delightfully innocent number to contrast with the comic. A half hour before the performances the costumes were miraculously ready and so was Lotta.

Although there was another show across the way, miners arrived filling Taylor's theater until it could hold no more.

Constance Rourke in her book *Troopers of the Gold Coast*, describes the night of Lotta's first real performance. "She seemed tireless, a tiny bubbling fountain of fun and quick life. On the rough stage with candles for footlights in the midst of smoke and shadows, she danced again and again; every other number was forgotten, even Taylor's dancing and singing. Then she appeared in her white dress with a round neck and puffed sleeves, and sang a plaintive, innocent ballad, looking like a pretty little red-haired doll."

The smoke-laden room reverberated with excitement and money rained upon the stage . . . quarters, half-dollars, huge Mexican dollars, a fifty-dollar gold slug and a scattering of nuggets. The camp at Rabbit Creek had rallied around Taylor in the contest with Dr. Robinson defeating the renowned producer who retired from Rabbit Creek leaving Mary Ann Crabtree to think upon her child's success.

Taylor was filled with excitement. He talked with Mrs. Crabtree of how much money could be made by a tour of the mining camps, how they needed more musicians, a violinist, and himself on the guitar. Mary Ann must learn to play the triangle. What could she say? She was carried along on the wave of her child's success. It was the opportunity she must have thought of many times, a way that she and Lotta could escape from John Crabtree's string of failures and she seized it.

There were days of intensive rehearsing and an almost ceaseless tap of feet on the dark boards of the hall as Mart Taylor taught Lotta a greater repertoire of dance steps and songs. One of her tenderest numbers was "How Can I Leave Thee?" a ballad Lotta trilled that for years would bring furtive wet tears down the most hardened miner's face.

A month after Dr. Robinson had departed, Mary Ann wrote a parting note for her husband to find when he returned from the most recent of his series of ventures.

Lotta toured the gold camps, both large and small.
Harper's New Monthly Magazine, 1858

She had finally made up her mind that she knew what was best and she and Lotta left Rabbit Creek with Taylor to tour the mining camps. They headed north to the camps of San Juan, Malakoff, Sixteen to One, Alleghaney, Camptonville, and Downieville. The greatest concentration of small mining camps was in the steep mountains north of Downieville.

"Why did God tilt this country straight up and down?" Lotta wondered as they wound around a tortuous trail on horseback. At first she had been afraid of horses but had come to love her little mare, Nina. It was hard work but Lotta was gaining valuable experience. They did not miss even a small camp. Her mother was firm when necessary, and coaxing if she needed to be in order to elicit the best possible performance from Lotta.

Mrs. Crabtree would play the triangle and sometimes do short imitations or monologues to round out the shows but it was Lotta the miners came to see . . . Lotta that they cheered . . . Lotta whose touching renditions made them

furtively wipe their eyes on their shirt sleeve as she sang
that summer and autumn, establishing a reputation in the
camps.

"When do we go to Grass Valley?" she would often ask
during the tour for she thought of it as "home," but there
were always more camps to visit until finally they reached
Oroville. One of the last stops was Grass Valley where they
would stay with old friends.

Lotta and her mother walked down the street to see the
house in which they had once lived and afterward the child
was determined to see her friend Lola's old home. The
picket fence had collapsed and the house was empty. It
appeared desolate indeed to Lotta and she felt sad as she
thought of the happy hours she had spent there learning
dances and songs and of how the sounds of talk and laughter
once radiated from the very walls.

The afternoon of the performance, she found herself
peering at each miner searchingly as if, under one of the
dusty, wide-brimmed hats, she might encounter the face of
Jonathon Moyle. Her eyes misted over and she couldn't bear
to think of his dying down in the darkness of the tunnels for
she had never forgotten the kindness of the big Cornishman
and his wondrous stories.

That night she gave one of the greatest performances of
her tour. Lotta danced again and again and the men roared
with pleasure. Money showered upon the stage, and to the
sound of thundering applause she at last closed with the
ballad, "How Can I Leave Thee?" Tears ran down the
cheeks of some of the miners crowded close around the
stage.

As she sang the last verse she looked out in the semi-
darkness and saw the crowd separating to make way for a
huge man lumbering toward her. Now, he was right in front

of the stage. At first she was frightened until she heard a deep, resonant voice.

"Lotta, my little Lotta. Do you remember me now that you are a star?"

"Jonathon! Is is really you? I feared you were dead in the mine."

"Dead? Not me, lass. I knew the cave-in was coming and headed into one of the slope tunnels."

"How did you know the mine was ready to cave-in?"

"Because up ahead o' it, I could hear 'em."

"Hear who, Jonathon? Who?"

"The Tommyknockers. They were just a tappin' and a tappin' on those wooden beams. They saved my life, lass. When I heard 'em, I knew what was comin' so I went into another tunnel to be safe. It took me a while to find a slope that led to the good fresh air. By the time I got out, and back to our story tellin' place, you and your mama were gone away."

"Tommyknockers really do help people, then?"

"They help those that will listen to them, Lotta." She hugged him fiercely and a cheer rose from the men around them.

Lotta's tours through the mining country continued . . . to Shasta and Weaverville and French Gulf, one of the wildest camps of them all. But Lotta had learned to handle the crowds of rough miners and she was to tour the gold camps of California again and again before she became a young woman.

Finally, the greatest challenge of all, a tour including New York and the East, was being planned by Taylor and Mrs. Crabtree when sad news arrived. Lola Montez had died. She was alone in New York at the time and virtually penniless. Lotta was filled with grief . . . if only she had gone with her, if she could somehow have helped her during those last days.

Preparations for her important tour were postponed and several weeks passed before she realized that high-spirited Lola would have wanted her to go and put on her best performances . . . for her!

Lotta conquered New York, but it was to San Francisco that she most often returned playing long engagements, making a gift of a fountain to the city she would always love best, and Lotta's Fountain is still there.

She never forgot California even after she became wealthy and retired to the East. Her mother had managed those Mexican dollars and Rabbit Creek nuggets well! Almost eighty when she died in 1924, Lotta's fortune was worth something over four million dollars and it was in character that she had bequeathed it to hundreds of charities.

If there was a key to her success, it was that Lotta Crabtree was a gifted entertainer able to charm rough miners and impress sophisticated New Yorkers simply by being herself. But she would always be known as the darling of the lonely men in the gold camps . . . who were often away from their loved ones for several years at a time.

She could make them forget their hardships, lift them out of their discouragement . . . she could make them laugh and she could make them cry. Lotta Crabtree was one of the great, warm, unforgettable figures of American pioneer history.

19.
The Bride of Vallecito

East of San Diego and not far beyond Descanso and Lassiters, is Vallecito . . . little valley, as its name implies. With the coming of the Butterfield stagecoach line in 1858, the town boomed and exhausted passengers on their way to the gold fields stared up at the low-lying purple mountains and the majestic Laguna range in the distance grateful to be approaching Vallecito. Their long trek from back east was nearly over.

Vallecito Stage Station, built in 1851 of sod and brown adobe brick, is today a desolate, abandoned place. The doorway of this ancient building now looms dark and gaping while everywhere there is eerie stillness. An arid landscape is covered profusely by silvery gray, leafless smoke trees, desert willows, and feathery bushes with pale green foliage. Even in the bright light of the noonday sun, the smoke tree has a ghostly look and at a distance resembles a mysterious cloud of vapor hovering just above the ground.

No longer do four and six mule teams swing with a flurry of dust across the Overland up to the Vallecito Stage Station. Nor will it ever again be the refuge for desert weary travelers it was a hundred years ago . . . for the old station is said to be haunted . . . cloaked in mystery. Of course, if violent events produced hauntings, enough took place at many stations like this, strung across the West, to supply them with ghosts forever. They were the scene of murders, brutal attacks, robberies, and diverse violent deaths.

A desertwise old man says that no one who knows the stories of Vallecito could ever sleep within these walls and, perhaps, he is right.

It was in 1858, when passengers first came West on the Butterfield Stage, that Eileen O'Connor left Louisville, Kentucky, with her Uncle William for the adventure of her life. She was on her way to Sacramento. Even the name of the distant California town had a glamorous ring to the excited and unsophisticated young girl whose fiancé had struck it rich in the gold fields. He had asked her to meet him there to be married.

Eileen had devoured *A Pocket Guide to California* and was convinced she would learn to rough it and adapt to the life of the mining camps. Nor was there anything to be apprehensive about for she dearly loved Frank Shaughnessy and he would take care of her when she got there.

"Travel in our luxurious coaches," the ads for the stages read. Now, at last there was a sure and easy route to California. The journey was long, but Eileen did not worry.

Her mother had lovingly helped her select her wardrobe of new dresses . . . a dark red coat and matching velvet hat that sat pertly on top of her thick chestnut hair and most exciting of all a beautiful, white silk wedding dress, trimmed with Belgian lace and sewn with the tiniest stitches imaginable. As she folded it before she left, she pressed the silk of the wedding gown against her cheek and her blue eyes sparkled.

Eileen and her uncle packed two baskets of food for the trip as everyone had heard that sometimes the places to stop were few and even when travelers arrived, if there were more people than usual, the inn or taverns were apt to run out. They left the last of September and by mid-October, one of the things Eileen was beginning to miss was fresh vegetables. A meal of cornbread, potatoes, and coffee became a feast. She had discovered quickly that mattresses at the inns were terrible, and sore from the constant jolts, she sometimes slept poorly. Worst of all were the bugs!

Cleanliness was another problem. She usually found a bowl and pitcher in the room and sometimes a tin tub, but often no water and would have to go to the pump and bring back bucketfuls to warm beside a fireplace. She carefully hoarded her meager supply of lye soap. As they traveled farther West, a roof over her head was a luxury for they were often forced to sleep on the ground under a tent.

In the same stage with Eileen and her uncle were two male passengers also headed for the gold fields. One was a man of the cloth, from the East named Reverend Frederick Fox, who after the first week ceased his pretense of bearing the discomforts of the trip cheerfully. A small, pasty faced man with straw-colored hair and stained teeth, his few smiles were directed at Eileen. Quite talkative for the first week, he must have divulged his entire personal history and Eileen tolerated his stories out of necessity, for in the close quarters of the coach there was no escape. She was thankful when he began to lapse into long silences.

The other passenger was an elegantly attired man in black who called himself Ronald Skinner. His eyes were dark agate marbles, completely devoid of warmth, and his smooth white hands with their well-kept nails gave the impression he was unaccustomed to any sort of manual work, but when he went about setting up camp his movements were quick and dextrous. His comments to Fox were becoming increasingly sarcastic for the man tried every pretext to evade his share of the work.

It was necessary to repair an axle and that held the stage up for almost a day ... then more delay when a stream usually forded with ease became impassable due to melting snow and the travelers had to camp overnight until the water subsided. On one occasion, they lost almost two days traveling one of the longest legs of their journey between stations.

Fox either spilled the last of the water or drunk it himself, no one knew which, and against his better judgment William drank from the stream while they waited allowing Eileen to do the same.

Ads for luxurious stagecoach travel to the West had failed to mention the possibility of Indian attacks. As they passed through an area of hills, boulders and tall brush the driver warned that if an attack should come, they were to drop down in the coach with drawn pistols and wait for the savages to get within a few feet before firing. No sign of emotion crossed Skinner's face but the Reverend Fox whitened visibly. Indians in this wild and desolate part of the country had a reputation for being bloodthirsty savages who delighted in murder and torture.

The next day about noon, a cloud of dust appeared upon the horizon and it was the sight they had most dreaded . . . a band of approaching Indians. Fox dived to the floor landing on top of Eileen's carpet bag filled with all her precious and irreplaceable toilet articles. Skinner sat immobile, his hand resting on his Wesson six-shooter, and when the coach slowed to a stop absolute pandemonium erupted with Indians shouting and gesticulating all around them.

At first it was impossible to tell whether they were hostile or friendly. But as the confusion lessened the driver and the chief were seen standing beside the stage talking and Eileen's uncle was relieved to observe that the Indians were offering to share water and welcome provisions with the frightened travelers.

By now the stagecoach had become a torture chamber with its hard seats and continual motion. Body muscles turned into unoiled straps rubbing aching ribs while heat, sand, and the stench of horses and perspiration overwhelmed the senses. Every stage station, regardless of how little it had to offer, was eagerly anticipated as a brief respite from the miseries of the road.

During this third week Fox became ill and, in his delirium, groaned and cried out in terror about dying in "this God-forsaken place." Skinner looked at him with disgust and abandoned the tent the pair had shared, moving in with the driver while the sick man tossed and turned rending the cold night air with his cries. Eileen's uncle was disturbed over the man's condition for he feared it might be the dread Asiatic cholera.

One morning a few days before the coach was to reach Vallecito, the driver went over to the Reverend's tent to rouse him but Frederick Fox did not wake up. There was nothing to do but leave the body at the stagecoach stop where they had spent the night and as they pulled away, his grave was being dug by the brother of the station's owner.

"I feel sorry for the poor man, uncle; will you write his family about his death?" asked Eileen and William O'Connor assured her he would do so. By now, Eileen herself was pale and exhausted from the hardships of travel and a poor diet. Not far from Vallecito she began to feel extremely cold although the day was a warm one. Her uncle brought out some Mandrake pills . . . gave her several and covered her with a blanket but she continued to suffer from cold although she did not shake nor have chills. O'Connor knew this was one of the signs of cholera.

She became more and more miserable. The driver stopped the stage and she got out beside the road, retching with nausea. Then she would lie back against the seat of the lurching coach, her face deathly pale, so weak she could scarce hold up her head. Her uncle's agitation was pathetic to behold, especially since the poor man now appeared to be feeling ill himself.

He had decided by the time the stage reached Vallecito that they must stop over there and stay for a few days, "so she may rest until she is better." But he, too, was already quite weak and that very night "his soul was required of him by his maker," as the driver put it when he told the other passengers next morning as they prepared to leave without Mr. O'Connor. His death was so sudden there had been no time for him to have the benefit of the last rites of the Catholic church.

Fortunately, he had paid a week in advance for a room for Eileen. Sick as she was, it was impossible to keep her in bed. The woman who had been brought in to take care of her told the story for years to all who would listen and her son told it after her . . . and this is the way it happened.

"I did my best to take care of her but I couldn't keep the poor girl in bed. She kept looking toward the door of the room and trying to get up, saying she recognized her bridegroom standing in the doorway.

"'He's here for me and it's almost time for the wedding,' she went on . . . over and over. Poor girl. It made the tears come to my eyes just to hear her talk like that. Weak as she was toward the end, somehow she would manage to get up out of that bed and try to dress.

"One night I waked and found her standing in the center of the room in a white wedding gown so beautiful, it fair took me breath away. The moonlight shone in from the window and fell full upon her face and my she was lovely, even with the effects of the illness. I rose and hurried to her . . . 'twas good I did for the poor thing pitched over into my arms, so weak and faint was she and the next morning she was dead."

"At least this was the story my mother told me," said the son "and she was at the station for years. I heard more stories than you can possibly imagine ... many full of wickedness and violence. I don't think I ever really believed them for years until I drove into Vallecito late one night when mother was near death and I went straight to the house to see her. After I left her I passed the old stage station.

"I was feeling pretty low and for some crazy reason I thought if I just stood out there in the night beside it for awhile, it might be the way it used to be when I was a boy. If I could feel that way again just for a few minutes it could help me deal with this, do you know what I mean? I parked my car at the front of the station, got out and leaned back against it thinking of all the sadness inside me ... and then for a little while out there in the night I might have been eighteen again, and Mom kidding with me the way she used to do.

"Then I saw a patch of moonlight move. What's unusual about that? Shadows move, moonlight doesn't ... at least not fast enough to see. And it wasn't just a small patch ... why, it must have been about two feet wide and five feet long. I probably should say high because to my amazement it was the figure of a girl in a long white dress ... not an ordinary dress but a beautiful wedding gown and it shone with a sort of radiance. She stood for a moment in the hole where the door had been in the old stage station and then ... she started toward me.

"More than anything, I wanted to run but for some reason I could not, and on she came. In a way, I suppose I just froze there. I had heard of the story of the White Ghost of Vallecito and now ... there she was. As she glided toward me I could see the outlines of a breathtakingly lovely woman. When she was within a few feet of me her face was so filled with light that it was almost blinding to look into it.

"She extended her arms to me in the most imploring way and . . . involuntarily . . . I reached out to her. At that moment I experienced an electrical shock so intense I pitched backward almost falling. There was a sharp sound like the crackle of lightning; and I recovered myself and was wrenching open the door of the car when another shock suddenly coursed through my entire body.

"This time there was something different about it as if warmth and life were pulsing through me . . . but filled with fear of the unknown I turned on the ignition and pressed the accelerator to the floor. A cloud of dust rose behind my old blue Ford.

"Next morning when I waked up all I could think of was my desire to tell mother what had happened. I hurried over to see her and my sister greeted me with weeping and the news that she was dead. They had called me but received no answer and decided to wait until morning. My mother's spirit must have left her body about the same time I was at the stage station and I had the strangest feeling that the warm sensation I had felt course through me may have been her last good-bye.

"Mother had been kind to the girl who died there. Perhaps, they were together again . . . for a moment . . . there at the old Vallecito station. In any event, I have no desire to return at night . . . not now . . . and probably never."

20.
The Mark of Black Bart

It was the morning of August 5, 1877, and in a small San Francisco hotel a cool breeze moved the white lace curtain at the window. With a slender, genteel hand a man named Charles Bolton drew it back and stared down into the street below.

Beneath the window of his room was a young couple arm in arm, obviously in love, and he found himself thinking of his wife in Hannibal, Missouri. Mary had been good looking in a dark-haired Irish peasant way, heavy of frame with milky white skin and blue eyes. But why had he ever married her? How she bored him with her constant reiteration of the obvious. She would follow him around the house repeating something that to him seemed so apparent it needed no answer, until, finally, in desperation he answered. Her conversation was like the cud of a cow, the most inconsequential details masticated beyond belief until bereft of color or texture.

He had been employed by a manufacturing firm and was far more brilliant than the owner's son. The owner was impressed and once said, "Charles, you will be my assistant before long," but he finally saw it would be the incompetent son instead. He was bitter about the time he had spent in an inferior position learning the business only to be passed over. Bolton convinced his wife that his fortune lay elsewhere, not in a place like Hannibal, and that much as he regretted it he would have to be away for a time.

There was a suffocating quality about living with Mary somewhat like the humid Missouri summers. He had proba-

247

bly done her a disservice by marrying her, but once married he considered himself a man who honored his obligation to family. Over the years he had written her each week in a vein similar to the words he had penned today.

Oh, my dear. How I do hope you may retain your health until I can come to you. . . . I hope you will not think or attribute my not coming home to any lack of desire on my part or lack of affection for any of you. The clouds look dark and gloomy and the real struggle of life is at hand, and I must meet it and fight it out.

Let come what will, I must see my own loved Mary and our loving children once more.

> Good night,
> Charles

These letters followed something of a formula. Always, he pled some imminent battle of the spirit that he must discharge bravely and held out the hope of his return to the bosom of his family in some dim, unspecified future.

Charles folded the letter and placed it in an envelope upon the brown marble-topped dresser. After breakfast he would post it, then go down and stroll along the bay. He secured the diamond pin in his tie, adjusted his heavy gold watch chain and when he had tilted his natty derby to a rakish angle, Bolton stood back and surveyed himself in the mirror. He was about five feet ten inches in height with luxuriant dark hair and a heavy, graying mustache. Broad shouldered and straight as an arrow, Charles Bolton was the sort of man both men and women looked at twice and sometimes it was hard to look away, especially if his gaze met theirs, for his piercing, brilliant blue eyes were the most compelling thing about him.

One would have taken him for a gentleman who had done well financially and was enjoying it. Elegantly turned out, his small cane in hand, Bolton emerged from the front door of the Webb House Hotel at 37 Second Street and stepped jauntily along carrying a packet of clothes under his arm. He would drop these at the California Laundry on his way to breakfast. "They'll be ready for you in the morning, sir," said Phineas Fergusson as he turned the clothes over to his son, Walter. Walter handed them to a Chinese employee who stood in the doorway of the large room in the back of the laundry.

Charles turned in the direction of one of his favorite haunts, William Pike's New York Bakery on Kearney near Clay Street. Certainly, he must have had a clear conscience since it was less than a block away from the Central Police Station in the old City Hall and was a favorite eating place for members of the force. Sometimes, he would linger over coffee with Officer Dave Scannell whom he regarded as "a devilish nice fellow."

"Charlie, mind if I join you?" asked a deep voice and Bolton looked up to see the tall figure of officer Scannell standing beside him.

"Help yourself," said Charlie.

"Didn't know whether you were in town or not. Your mine's somewhere up in Nevada, right?"

"Yes, near the California line."

"How's the gold mining business?

"We've got some hard working Cornishmen on the job and my partners say, we'll make a fortune yet. What's your news?" Scannell's expression became one of perplexity.

"Did you hear about the stage coach robbery?"

Bolton was horrified. "Dave, that's terrible! Where?"

"A place in the hill country along the Russian River between Point Arenas and Duncan's Mills. A fellow stepped out from behind a hill into the path of the stage and shouted, 'Throw down the box!' "

"Great heavens! What did the bandit look like?"

"He had on a long linen duster. His head was covered with a flour-sack and he was holding a double-barreled shotgun. Of course, the driver threw down the box."

"How much did he get?"

"Not much, I think it was about three hundred dollars."

"No clues at all?"

"Oh, the driver said he had a deep, hollow voice. That's not much to go on. How many men have a deep, hollow voice, eh?"

"Well, I do for one," said Bolton, "and so do you, Dave." He smiled broadly, a glint in his bright blue eyes.

"Wait! I almost forgot. The posse that went out did find a clue and you won't believe what it was."

"What was it?"

"It was a poem. Imagine this scoundrel robbing a stage and then having the gall to leave a poem behind him."

"Ah, then his handwriting can be traced."

"Not much of a chance there . . . he wrote each line in different handwriting."

"Clever rascal! Was the poem any good?"

"Any good? Charlie, I don't sit around reading Shakespeare so I wouldn't know about that. They found it written on the back of a waybill just as the blackguard meant for them to."

"Well, what did it say?" said Charles.

"Let's see if I rightly remember." Scannell leaned back and lit a cigar. His eyes narrowed as he tried to recall the words. Bolton fidgeted a bit impatiently.

"Yes?"

"I have it! Here's the way it went.

> "I've labored long and hard for bread,
>   For honor and for riches,
>   But on my corns too long you've tred
>   You fine-haired sons of bitches."

"What language! What impudence! This man must be brought to justice."

"Yes. You know he even had the nerve to sign it."

"With his name?"

"He signed it 'Black Bart' and then wrote underneath it 'PO8.' "

"You don't mean he really thinks he's a poet. Will you be able to find him?" David was rising to his feet to leave. "There'll be dragnets and we'll get him. Take care of yourself, Charlie." Bolton nodded.

But finding the robber-poet was not to be that easy, for the trail was cold as a stone and there were ten thousand men in California with deep voices and shotguns. Nor would three hundred dollars in currency be easy to trace.

Charles Bolton stood on the wharf enjoying the bright, blue sky over the bay and glorying in the beauty of the day. He stared at San Quentin prison across the sparkling water thinking . . . poor devils! Bolton pulled a breakfast roll out of the pocket of his nattily tailored jacket, turned the pocket inside out emptying it meticulously of crumbs and, tearing the bread into small pieces, began to feed the raucous, squawking gulls.

Among the people who passed him enjoying the cool San Francisco July day was a woman rolling a carriage, and he raised his hat giving the baby an appreciative look. She paused and Bolton tucked in a corner of the blanket with a flattering comment.

After she walked on, his blue eyes misted over as his thoughts turned to the early years of his own family. He adored children and he missed watching them grow up most of all. Had it not been for his interests here in the West, he would have made more trips back home just to see them. But there wasn't much for a man of his sort back East. He wouldn't be happy keeping his nose to the grindstone in an office day in and day out. That wasn't for him.

No more was heard of "Black Bart" for almost a year. Then, high in the Sierra Mountains, in the green-walled canyon of the foaming Feather River, Black Bart appeared. As the stage was rolling along from Quincy to Oroville on the afternoon of July 28, 1878, on the long approach to a slow and difficult turn, he watched from the underbrush ahead looking through his binoculars. He instantly identified it as a Wells Fargo Stagecoach and when he did a thrill of excitement hurtled through every cell in his body.

To Black Bart this was like riding a fast horse and winning a race was to another, and that first sighting of the Wells Fargo stage was an unbearably sweet moment. The question of whether he would win the battle of wits and carry off the gold this time, may have raced through his mind.

The stage driver saw a figure masked by a flour sack and leveling a shotgun at him step out from the brush.

"Throw down the box," called out a deep, resonant voice. And the driver did as he was told. "All right. Be on your way!" shouted the bandit at the frightened man and with a wrenching jerk the stage lurched forward leaving a cloud of dust behind it. This time the bandit made a better haul than his earlier robbery. Breaking open the treasure box he found almost four hundred dollars in cash, a diamond ring, and a silver watch. He also robbed the mail and as he left he knew all this would buy time to enjoy long walks along the magnificent coast, months of the leisurely lifestyle he so relished in this delightful climate, and dining at the best restaurants. It was unfortunate that a man had to take such risks to live in the manner suited to him.

When officers arrived at the scene, in addition to the empty box they once again found a poem.

> Here I lay me down to sleep
> To wait the coming morrow,
> Perhaps success, perhaps defeat,
> And everlasting sorrow.
> Let come what will I'll try it on,
> My condition can't be worse;
> And if there's money in that box
> Tis money in my purse!

Again each line was written in a different hand to confuse his pursuers. An angry Governor announced a reward of $300 for Black Bart's capture and conviction. Wells Fargo added another $300 and the postal authorities sweetened the pot by contributing $200 more. Although the price on his head was now $800 the bandit grew ever more daring.

Bolton and his friend, Scannell, were drinking coffee again at William Pike's New York Bakery one morning talking about the fact that the hold-ups had gone on for some time now. Scannel did not seem nearly so confident as in the past. "Charles, we aren't even close to catching him.

He's here one day and fifty miles away the next." Charles shook his head and made a solicitous sound.

Twice in October there were stage robberies in the north by a single bandit wearing the flour sack disguise. One sheriff succeeded with the help of expert trackers in trailing the man for sixty miles. They lost the trail but Wells Fargo detective, J. B. Hume, now had something to go on and he was a bloodhound of a man. Convinced that someone in that part of the country must have seen him and be able to describe him, he finally met a farm woman up near Eel River who had taken in a gentlemanly tourist. The tourist had been on foot.

The woman's daughter had observed their visitor very closely. The stranger's coat sleeve had been slightly ripped and mended with white thread; he had graying brown hair, thinning above the forehead with wedges of baldness at the temples. She was not sure but thought two or three of his front teeth were missing and he had piercing blue eyes and hands that were slender and smooth, as if unaccustomed to hard work. Her mother added that he had carried on an intellectual and entertaining conversation and he reminded her of a preacher.

Mr. Hume went back to San Francisco thinking that for the first time he at least had a description of someone to look for. Perhaps, the man was "Black Bart," perhaps not. He was to spend the next five years finding out.

Six months would go by without a robbery and then there might be one a week. San Francisco officer, Scannell, had no leads on the bandit he had thought would be captured so soon. He had talked with the Wells Fargo man, Hume, from time to time but he was contemptuous of Hume's ideas that Black Bart could easily be recognized because he was a man who liked to drink coffee and held his newspaper at arm's length to read it when he didn't have his glasses on. That might be true of himself or any of a number of men on the force and he told Charlie Bolton as much.

"Keep this dry. I probably shouldn't be showing it to someone not on the force," said Scannell, reaching into his pocket and handing Bolton a four-page circular that the Wells Fargo people and police carried. "I won't breathe it to a soul," promised Charlie as he read the circular with great interest," and, I'll certainly keep my eyes skinned for this fellow."

For reasons of their own Wells Fargo had ordered their agents not to post it. The circular listed sixteen robberies, the flour sack he always wore over his head and his habit of jumping out in front of the team and stooping down so that he was shielded by the horses. It also described his politeness to passengers and the fact that he was always on foot. Then there were the details given by the daughter at the home where the stranger had shared a meal with them, describing him as having gray hair, light eyes, a gray mustache, and chin whiskers. Charlie handed the circular back. He had the feeling Dave either didn't like Hume or was a little jealous of him.

"This fellow never fires a shot, Charlie. He just levels his gun and sometimes the stage drivers don't even wait for him to speak, they're so scared. They just throw down the box and gallop on. But some day a chance event is going to trip him up, and we'll get him."

"You're right, Dave. That's the way it goes."

"Is your gold mine doing all right?"

"Well, it could be better, but now and then we strike a good vein. Trouble is pay dirt always seems to run out."

"If you can just let me know ahead, it would help me to get out of the city and rest for a couple of weeks in good company."

"You go off now and then to see family, don't you Dave?"

"It's not the same. I usually try to lend a hand when I'm there."

"I'll keep that in mind, Dave. Guess we could feed you some che-muck up there!"

"Miner's food, eh," said Scannell smiling. "Sure, I'll try it."

The next morning when Bolton went to the laundry to get his clothes, Dave Scannell came in to pick up his shirts. The pair stood at the counter together waiting and the Chinese employee came out with Bolton's first. "Mistair Bolton. I mendee your coat. You likee?" He proudly showed him the place and Bolton thanked him giving some extra money to the man, "Yes, yes. It's fine." Bolton and Scannell walked toward the New York Bakery but they didn't have coffee together for Charlie had "an appointment with a possible investor in the mine." "I'm really not much of a coffee drinker, Dave," said Bolton . . . Scannell gave him a surprised glance . . . "It's just a good spot to talk."

Bolton now found himself beginning to sleep very poorly at the Webb Hotel where he had stayed for so many years. It was the last of October, bleak and rainy with long, cold nights, and Charles Bolton waked often with pictures of the California countryside passing through his restless mind.

Around San Francisco the hills of summer were smooth rounded golden mounds all rising at different angles from each other and with little underbrush to conceal their contours. But soon they would be fresh and green from the fall rains. In those hills there were a thousand folds and crevices that could provide a place to hide, gullies that twisted and turned and sometimes made a trail known only to one whose eye had marked it.

On November 3, 1888, at Reynolds Ferry, Reason Mc-
Connell, driver for the stage company, rose early. This was
the day he always went to Copperopolis and today he had to
make a connection at Milton and a special stop at Tuttletown. It was cold enough to wear his mackinaw coat and
still pitch black as the stage rolled out of Sonora before
sunrise. There were no passengers, and the heavy box
fastened to the floor of the stage was the reason for the stop
at Tuttletown. In it were 228 ounces of amalgam from the
mill at the Patterson Mine and six hundred dollars worth of
gold.

At Tuttletown "Grandma Rolleri" owned a small hotel
and the ferry. This was before she had bought the Calaveras
Hotel over at Angels Camp. A big, plump woman with a
warm smile, and dark brown hair painted with broad
streaks of gray, "Grandma" was popular throughout the
gold region; and since she was widowed she depended
heavily on the help of her son, Jimmy, who operated the
ferry.

"How 'bout if I ride along with you today?" Jimmy asked
McConnell. The driver hesitated.

"Don't know as it'd do any harm. Hoist yourself up along-
side me."

"Wait a minute 'til I get my rifle. Maybe, I can bag us a
rabbit or even a deer." The boy and the driver were good
friends and McConnell was glad to have someone to talk to.
Jimmy might even bring down some rabbits with that Henry
repeating rifle of his. When the boy came back with his rifle
he had a tin mug full of hot coffee for his friend and a bear
sign resting on top of it.

"Your ma's doughnuts are mighty good," said McConnell, biting into it.

"Git up here on this seat and tell me who's been stayin' at your hotel."

"Had a few peddlers and about a week ago the niftiest sort of man. He was walkin' and he stayed overnight to rest. That man knew so much I could have listened to him for a year. I hated that he was only stayin' one night. Ferried him across the next mornin' and we talked all the way. I can see him now, walking off, his blanket-roll under his arm."

"What was his name?"

"Dogged, if I remember. Then there was Mr. Hume. He stops with us pretty frequent. You know him, don't you?"

"Yep. Guess he was snoopin' around lookin' to get Black Bart and if ever anybody catches him, I'd say it 'ud be J. B. Hume. That man don't quit once he gets started."

"He won't catch Black Bart. Nobody can," said Jimmy.

"Black Bart wouldn't bother me none. I'd just reach down at my feet fast as a flash, grab my six-shooter and that 'ud be the end of him," said McConnell with a wink. Jimmy looked admiringly at his friend.

"I think he must be a fast draw, Mr. McConnell."

"They all are until the day they meet their match, son, and that 'ud be me," said McConnell, giving his waterfall of a mustache a confident tug.

"I'd almost hate to see him shot dead. They say he's a mighty polite man. Why, one time he threw a woman passenger's purse right back to her."

"Sure he did. He doesn't want some woman's purse. Black Bart wants the Wells Fargo box and the United States mail."

"I just meant he tries to be decent."

"It's decent to take checks and gold that don't belong to you?" He was a mite provoked. Jimmy shook his dark mane of brown hair.

"Guess not. I just don't know as I like that man, Hume. He kind of gives me the willies." McConnell didn't answer. He was glad no one knew about that gold in the box and that he was almost at his destination. The pair didn't talk for awhile. Jimmy was content to be on his way to Copperopolis.

"You a pretty good shot, kid?" McConnell asked, nodding his head toward the rifle.

"Throw a buffalo in his tracks," replied Jimmy with a grin.

"Get 'em with that first shot to the brain or the neck, eh."

"Yep."

Black Bart had now become a legend. Between 1875 and 1883, twenty-seven California stage drivers saw the masked man and knew him for the state's most famous bandit. All of them halted their horses and obeyed when he called out, "Throw down the box." Californians read newspaper reporters' accounts of Black Bart's exploits, laced with colorful exaggerations, and were intrigued by the verse he boldly left behind.

No clues were found in the surrounding area after any of the robberies for he seemed to vanish as suddenly as he had appeared. It was clear that the bandit was a man who could not be caught. One day he was here and another he was miles away. The law never found his trail, much less came close to him.

The road McConnell was driving was one of the main stage routes and passengers would change at Milton to go to Stockton where they could catch a train or board a riverboat for San Francisco. Jimmy grew restless as they approached Funk Hill.

"Why don't I take a cut-off on foot and find some small game in the brush?"

"Well, git up an' dust then, lad. I'll meet you on the other side."

There were no hills and no bad turns, just straight road. Reason McConnell was approaching Funk Hill now and the horses began breathing heavily as they pulled the coach. Just as he crested it, he heard the snap of twigs and a stirring in the brush beside him.

The driver swung around and found himself staring straight into the steel gray muzzle of a shotgun. The man holding the gun on him wore a flour sack with two eye holes over his head and there was no doubt in McConnell's mind that it was Black Bart. He felt a shiver of real fear.

"Stop the stage," came the terse command. McConnell stopped.

"Who was the man who got out on the other side of the hill?"

"He was just a boy ridin' with me lookin' to round up some stray cattle in the switches," answered McConnell.

"Get down."

If he didn't he was certain to be shot but if he took his foot off the brake on the hill, the brakes were worn and the stage might begin to roll backward.

"I'm afraid the stage will roll back down," said McConnell.

"Not if it has rocks behind the wheels," said the bandit and he kicked some under it keeping McConnell covered.

"Now. Loose the horses from stage." The driver obeyed instructions. As he unbuckled the straps, he wondered when Jimmy would appear with his rifle. Would the boy be shot by the bandit and possibly killed?

"Take those horses with you, go down to the bottom of the other side of this hill and stay there . . . if you don't want to be hurt," ordered the bandit. There was a rustle in the underbrush near Black Bart and McConnell's heart pounded hard as a runaway horse's hoofs. If Jimmy walked out of that brush he would be killed. They both heard the rustle the second time and looked toward the side of the road. A rabbit bounded out of the brush and across in front of the stage.

"Don't just stand there! Take those horses and do as I say."

As McConnell walked down the hill he heard one heavy blow after another and knew the bandit was breaking into the box bolted to the floor inside the stage. This was a different situation for Black Bart, not as easy as when it was up front and he could simply say. "Throw down the box!" Then it took only a short time to break into it, rip the mail sacks open and be on his way.

When the driver reached the bottom of the hill he stood there wishing he really did have that six-shooter he had bragged about using. He would have made Black Bart jump a lot of dust. But where had that boy got to? he was worried for fear he would hear the pounding and head in that direction thinking something was wrong with the stage. It was time for him to be coming through the brush to meet him. Then something moving on the hillside caught his eye and it was Jimmy. McConnell raised his arm and gestured to him to keep back away from the road as he came down to join him. When he did, they quietly moved up the road toward the top of the hill.

"Jimmy, aim that gun at him and if he runs, shoot. Don't give me that look . . . I said shoot him!"

When they reached the top of the hill, Bart was just backing out of the stagecoach and he didn't stop. For some reason Jimmy made no move to raise his rifle. McConnell grabbed the gun shooting twice but missing each time.

"Give it here. I'll get him, but I ain't a'goin' to kill him," said Jimmy and taking the rifle he shot and wounded him. Bart stumbled, but kept on running and soon disappeared, somewhere out there in the brush. McConnell hitched up the horses and they road off to Copperopolis to report the robbery.

"Mr. McConnell."

"Yes."

"That's the man that stopped with us for a night, the one that was so nice to me."

"That be why you didn't shoot for so long?" Jimmy didn't reply.

Wells Fargo wired to San Francisco for J. B. Hume's assistant, Wells Fargo detective, John Thacker and to San Andreas for Sheriff Ben Thorne. Sheriff Thorne arrived at the scene wearing his "Buckeye" Stetson, the highest, widest, and handsomest hat of them all. But Thorne was a real professional. He organized the posse and set them combing the hillside; and he was the one who found some of the bandit's belongings cached behind a big rock. The gunshot wound and his pursuers had kept him from picking up two pairs of shirt cuffs, a black derby hat, an empty binoculars case, and a white handkerchief.

Detective Johnny Thacker interviewed McConnell and also Jimmy Rolleri.

"Jimmy, you wounded Black Bart and because of that, I think we're going to get him much quicker. You're a good shot."

"I hope so, sir."

"Did you get a good look at the fellow?"

"Only for a second. He turned and saw us just before he ran."

"Have you ever seen him before?" There was no answer.

"Jimmy, that was Black Bart. At least we think he was the one who held a gun on the stage. Now, if your friend McConnell hadn't done what he told him to, he might be dead."

"Well, he was the fellow who stayed with us overnight at the inn about two weeks ago."

"Tell me exactly what he looked like."

"He was about five foot ten, kind of slight build, brown hair with gray at the temples, a gray mustache and the brightest blue eyes I ever saw. He told me stories about all the different gold camps and the people, even said he'd met John Sutter; but he seemed to like to listen to me, too." Jimmy had noticed the man's smooth hands when he gave him his room key and known he wasn't a miner.

"We don't usually have people ask for a key to their room. That got me interested and that's when we set to talkin'."

"Where do you think he went after the robbery?"

"Why, how would I know that? Maybe he found a stream and was able to wash the blood off, then . . . rest in some rincon or sheltered place."

This time Bart had broken his cardinal rule which was never to stay overnight near the site of one of his robberies. Before he went to the Rolleri Hotel he must have visited the Patterson mine at Tuttletown and learned of the shipment. He had used his knowledge of mining as a way to make friends, perhaps with the owner, Dr. Drake, or one of the miners. His stay in the area and his friendship with the boy, probably about the age of one of his own children, proved his downfall. When Thacker returned to San Francisco and reported the interview with Jimmy to J. B. Hume, it matched Hume's earlier description of Black Bart from the mother and daughter.

The first clue found that might lead to his whereabouts was in the contents of the package Thacker brought back with him from Sheriff Thorne. A derby hat, two pairs of cuffs, and a handkerchief were among the items. In the corner of the white handkerchief was the mark "F.X.0.7," a San Francisco laundry mark used to identify each customer. Black Bart had only one week of freedom left.

A Wells Fargo detective began to go down a list of laundries in San Francisco calling on each one with the pretext that he was trying to trace an old friend. Several days passed before he reached the laundry agency of Mr. Ware at 316 Bush Street. Ware looked at his records and found the mark F.X.0.7.

"Why that's Charlie Bolton. Always wears a derby hat and carries a little cane. You won't meet a nicer gentleman. Let's see. I believe you can find him at his hotel, the Webb."

Charlie Bolton was arrested that afternoon as he was sauntering down Bush Street near the hotel. Wells Fargo evidence helped convict Bolton, alias Black Bart, and he was sent to San Quentin Prison on the island in the bay. He served his time, was heard of and interviewed occasionally, and then one day he disappeared . . . never to be seen in San Francisco again.

He was reported farther south in Modesto, Merced, Madera, and finally in Visalia but there the trail ended. In March of 1888, J. B. Hume received a bundle, via Wells Fargo, from a hotel in Visalia with a note that the valise in the bundle had never been called for by a guest who had said he would be coming back to pick it up. The hotel clerk thought Hume might be interested. Inside the valise were two pairs of shirt cuffs with the laundry mark "F.X.0.7," two neckties, small paper packages of crackers, sugar, pickles, coffee, and a jar of currant jelly.

On the following July 27 the stage from Bieber to Redding was held up by one man, on November 8 the stage from Downieville to Nevada City was similarly robbed and a gold bar taken worth well over a thousand dollars. Hume went up to investigate. He came back convinced the hold-ups were the work of Black Bart and on November 14, 1888, he issued a brand new circular. Two weeks later the stage from Eureka to Ukiah was robbed.

When the robberies suddenly stopped an unusual rumor started. The rumor was that Wells Fargo had decided to pay Black Bart a salary for life, so their stages would be safe!

There are few men of whom so many different stories have been told. Between 1875 and 1883, twenty-eight, bold, swaggering stagecoach drivers saw the masked man. Each of the twenty-eight halted his sweating horses, calmed his terrified passengers as much as possible and with a double-barrelled shotgun aimed at his breast handed over the loot. Black Bart became one of the most elusive and mysterious figures of the gold mines era.

Wells Fargo gave a specially made Winchester rifle to Jimmy and on its silver plate was engraved "James Rolleri, Jr., For Meritorious Conduct, November 3, 1883." Jimmy died in 1903, but his sisters continued to display the rifle on the wall of the Calaveras Hotel in Angel Camp, California, until the hotel was destroyed by fire in 1938. A few Californians are still left who stayed at the old Calaveras and remember the handsome rifle.